The *Wedding of*

_____ ✎

and

_____ ✎

on

_____ ✎

The Classic Bride

Style, Poise, and Grace . . . Under Pressure

The Classic Bride

Style, Poise, and Grace . . . Under Pressure

Edited by Andrea Mattei
With contributions from Shelly Hagen,
Janet Anastasio, Michelle Bevilacqua, Stephanie Peters,
Laura Morin, Emily Ehrenstein, Barbara Cameron,
Jennifer Jenkins, and Jennifer Lata Rung.

SWEET WATER PRESS

Published by Adams Media, an F+W Publications Company
57 Littlefield Street
Avon, MA 02322

ISBN: 1-59337-572-7

Printed in China by Global PSD

J I H G F E D C B A

Contains portions of material adapted and abridged from *The Everything® Wedding Book, 3rd Edition* by Shelly Hagen, © 2004, Adams Media; *The Everything® Wedding Book, 2nd Edition* by Janet Anastasio, Michelle Bevilacqua, and Stephanie Peters, © 2000, Adams Media; *The Everything® Wedding Organizer* by Laura Morin, © 1997, Adams Media; *The Everything® Wedding Checklist, 2nd Edition* by Janet Anastasio and Michelle Bevilacqua, © 2001, Adams Media; *The Everything® Wedding Etiquette Book, 2nd Edition* by Emily Ehrenstein and Laura Morin, © 2001, Adams Media; *The Everything® Wedding Vows Book, 2nd Edition* by Janet Anastasio and Michelle Bevilacqua, © 2001, Adams Media; *The Everything® Weddings on a Budget Book* by Barbara Cameron, © 2002, Adams Media; *The Everything® Wedding Shower Book* by Jennifer Jenkins, © 2000, Adams Media; and *The Everything® Creative Wedding Ideas Book* by Jennifer Lata Rung, © 2003, Adams Media.

This publication is designed to provide accurate and authoritative information with regard to the subject matter covered. It is sold with the understanding that the publisher is not engaged in rendering legal, accounting, or other professional advice. If legal advice or other expert assistance is required, the services of a competent professional person should be sought.

—From a *Declaration of Principles* jointly adopted by a Committee of the American Bar Association and a Committee of Publishers and Associations

Director of Manufacturing: Susan Beale • Associate Director of Production: Michelle Roy Kelly • Associate Managing Editor: Laura M. Daly • Project Manager: Jason Flynn • Project Editor: Andrea Mattei • Cover design: Frank Rivera • Interior design: Colleen Cunningham • Interior layout: Barb Karg • Divider layout and design: Stephanie Lombardi • Prep/Prepress: Matt LeBlanc

Divider photographs in order of appearance: ©2001 Corbis Corporation, ©2000 Getty Images, Inc. ©2001 Corbis Corporation, ©2001 Corbis Corporation, ©2000 Getty Images, Inc. , ©2000 Getty Images, Inc.

CONTENTS

INTRODUCTION

*C*ongratulations on your engagement! You're going to get married. Take a moment to soak this all in. After all, your upcoming wedding is probably a day you've been dreaming about from the time you were a little girl. You have cause to celebrate and revel in this wonderful time—you've found the right guy, and you're ready to take this big step and start your life together as husband and wife. You're also about to embark on a wedding-planning journey that can be at once exciting and overwhelming as you pull together all of the details for your big day.

You're going to have a lot to do, and you're also going have a lot of questions along the way. Don't fret—this chic, elegant planner has all of the strategies and tips a polished bride like you needs to stay calm, cool, and collected. Imagine Audrey Hepburn's flawless style mixed with the no-nonsense, get-the-job-done attitude of "The Apprentice." What's better than that? You can take your organizer with you anywhere, and it will help you to steer through any prenuptial planning pressure that comes your way. Use it to help you plan wisely—the more you stay organized, the less stress you will have during the course of your wedding process, and the less stress you have, the more you will enjoy every minute of it!

The key to arriving at the wedding day you've always wished for is taking one small, smart step at a time. To help you toward that goal, this organizer is broken down into three parts with six main sections that will lead you through everything from announcing your engagement and setting up a workable schedule, to keeping all of the last-minute details in check so you can breathe a sigh of relief as your big day gets underway. Inside, you'll find budget worksheets, a to-do checklist with a workable timeline, question lists so you know exactly what to ask every last vendor, tips to help you stay cool under pressure, and more.

Use all of these tools to get off on an organized foot now, and you'll reap the benefits later. You won't be able to avoid every pitfall, but you'll remain poised and prepared as decisions have to be made and issues present themselves. And, as every classic bride knows, grace under pressure is everything!

It's Official

In This Section:

Beginning Stages

Announcing Your Engagement

Getting Organized

Setting Your Date

Making Schedules

Chapter One

beginning stages

Once you are officially engaged, you'll want to share the happy news with everyone you know, and even people you don't. But there's more to do than all that gushing, and getting organized is a must.

Announcing Your Engagement

Before you start shouting from the rooftops, think about it. There is a certain protocol to all of this, after all. By the way, this might be the right time to mention that you and the beastly protocol burden are going to butt heads now and then during the course of your wedding planning. It's worth noting that although you don't have to bow to protocol simply for tradition's sake all the time, there are times when following protocol will help you to stay courteous, save feelings, and keep things running smoothly. This is one of those instances.

Who Hears the News First?

For starters, just think about how your parents or your fiancé's parents would feel if they weren't the first to hear about your engagement. Announce your engagement right away to both sets of parents—in person, if possible. If one or both sets of parents lives too far for you to take a spur-of-the-moment road trip out there, then tell them on the phone, and make sure you call them before you start spreading the news to anyone else in person. Then, if you can, try to plan a visit soon afterwards to celebrate in person. If both sides of the family have yet to meet, the early engagement period is a good time to do some "getting to know you;" so see if you can get one set of parents to tag along on the trip so everyone can get acquainted.

In addition to the parents, children are the other most important factor to consider. If either you or your groom has children from a previous marriage, make sure you fill them in on what's happening right away. Your impending marriage is a major life-changing event for them, too; don't let them hear about it from someone else! Because a parent's new marriage can be stressful for children, it's important to give them all the reassurance they need. Try to sense and quell their fears, and make them as much a part of the wedding as the situation allows.

After you've told these VIPs, continue through the line of announcement protocol. Grandparents are obviously tops on the list, as are siblings, followed by aunts, uncles, and cousins you are close to, as well as your closest friends. From there, you can spread the word with coworkers and other personal acquaintances. If you already know who your attendants will be, by all means, waste no time in asking them. But there's also no harm done if you wait a little while on this. (Just make sure you don't wait too long; be considerate and give your attendants plenty of advanced notice.)

Your Announcement in Print

Although not absolutely necessary, one quick and easy way to make even more people aware of your impending nuptials is via a newspaper announcement. Traditionally, the parents of the bride often placed this announcement, but these days, either set of parents, or the couple themselves can take care of this. Information is usually sent to the lifestyle or society editor of your local newspaper, but call just to make sure. Also ask about fees while you're at it; this isn't unusual these days, especially because many newpapers are deluged with so many marriage announcements. Although all newspapers have their own time frames for printing engagement announcements, usually they don't like to print them more than one year prior to the wedding.

A typical engagement announcement includes the names of the bride and groom and a little bit about them (where they are from, where they live, and where they went to college, for instance), their parents' names, and the wedding date. Many couples include an engagement photo, too.

If either or both families live in another state, send them a copy of the photo and information, so they can arrange for an announcement in their local paper as well.

Your Engagement Party

Just a quick note on this before you dive into the serious scheduling and planning details: Although the bride's family traditionally hosted an engagement party, it's perfectly acceptable for the groom's family (or anyone else) to do the honors. You can even plan this celebration on your own if you'd like. Since you'll have enough other formalities on your mind as you plan the actual wedding, you can and should have as informal an engagement party as you'd like. Phone invites or handwritten notes will do just fine. You can have the party at home, in a casual hall, or in a restaurant, depending on how many people you're inviting.

If someone throws an engagement party for you, show your appreciation by sending a thank-you note and perhaps bringing them a small gift. One more word to the wise and classy bride: Friends and family will likely start showering you with gifts at your engagement party. Stay on top of things and send prompt thank-you notes!

Getting Organized

After you've shared your big news with everyone and you've celebrated your upcoming marriage, it's time to get down to business. Before you even consider meeting with caterers, making an appointment with your chosen officiant, or venturing into a bridal salon, take a trip to the office supply store first. Yes, that's right—head to Staples, Office Max, Wal-Mart, or wherever else you can get your hands on some basic organizational tools.

This small-scale planner is what you'll take with you when you're out and about. It's great for taking to appointments and storing your fabric swatches. But eventually, you're going to need more space, and that calls for a large-sized, expandable filing system you can store at home with all of your wedding information in one place. These basic items are inexpensive and easy to find, and they'll prove incredibly useful. Here are some supplies to stock up on:

- A sturdy three-ring binder (the *fattest* one you can find, so you'll have room to fit all your paperwork).

- Removable section dividers.

- File tabs to label each section.

- Folders you can insert in your binder to hold receipts, samples, and other loose items.

- A three-hole puncher to punch holes in all your contracts, brochures, and lists, so you can insert them into your binder.

- Small sticky tabs in various colors, to flag important items.

Once you've got all your supplies, separate your binder into sections for each of the major planning areas, including:

- Budget
- Guest List
- Ceremony

- Band/DJ
- Transportation
- Dresses/Tuxes

- Reception/Catering
- Photographer
- Videographer

- Jewelry, Hair, Makeup
- Marriage License
- Honeymoon

Set this system up right, and be faithful about inserting all pertinent details. Your wedding binder is also a great place to store creative ideas you have for your wedding.

Get used to carrying your *Classic* planner with you everywhere you go, but also keep up with extended details in your larger binder. These things will be your lifeline—and your ticket to pre-wedding tranquility—when you need it most.

Making Schedules

As soon as you start your planning, you'll be swimming in details, so the faster you get moving, the better. Depending on the type and size of your wedding, you might have lots to do—or tons to do. Whatever the case, you'll have a hard time getting *any* of it done without a reliable schedule.

A solid timeline will keep you from getting confused—and over-whelmed. Take it month by month. Here's a general idea of what needs to be done, and when you should be doing it.

Poised Under Pressure: **Put Your Man to Work**

Wedding planning isn't a one-woman show—you'll need help, especially from your fiancé. One way to drum up more enthusiastic participation from your husband-to-be is to help him find tasks that suit his talents. He'll be a lot happier about helping if he's doing something he enjoys. For example, if your guy's a math whiz, let him keep track of the budget. Or, if he's the creative type, turn him loose to invent some clever wedding favors.

As soon as possible, set the basics in place.

❑ Announce your engagement.

❑ Decide on what kind of wedding you want: big or small, formal or casual, and so on.

❑ Consider the time of year, day of the week, and time of day you prefer for your wedding.

❑ Decide on your budget.

❑ Set the date and book the locations for the ceremony and reception.

Once you decide on where you're having the ceremony and reception, you have some other hefty choices to make. Yes, this is some of the hard stuff, but don't sweat it. Once you deal with these big things, you can rest a little easier, as other details will fall into place.

Nine to Twelve Months Before the Wedding

❑ Meet with your officiant.

❑ If you're having an engagement party, set a date and buy your invitations.

❑ Start working on your preliminary guest list.

❑ Choose your wedding party (also consider any other special roles you'd like certain people to play in your wedding).

❑ Hire a consultant, if you're planning to do so.

❑ Take an engagement photo and contact newspapers to place an engagement announcement.

❑ Consult with and select a photographer.

❑ Meet with and select a caterer, if necessary.

❑ Meet with and decide on a DJ or band.

- Meet with and select a florist; begin discussing options.
- Discuss transportation to ceremony and reception.
- Decide if you want a videographer; if so, choose one.
- Begin researching and planning any special ethnic or family customs you want to incorporate into your wedding.
- Sign all the vendor contracts and send in deposits.
- If you feel it's necessary, check into wedding insurance options.

Brides: Begin shopping for your gown; you should make a final decision eight or nine months before the wedding.

Six to Eight Months Before the Wedding

- Plan your color scheme.
- Brides: Start shopping with bridesmaids for their dresses; order them no less than six months in advance.
- Select and order your headpiece, shoes, and jewelry.
- Start planning the honeymoon.
- Begin looking for invitations; finalize your selection at least four months in advance.
- Finalize your guest list.
- Start choosing gifts for your bridal registry.
- Reserve a block of hotel rooms for out-of-town guests.
- Continue planning ceremony and reception details.
- Discuss menu selections with your reception facility director/caterer.
- Start looking into your ceremony music.
- Start planning your rehearsal dinner.

Four to Five Months Before the Wedding

❏ Grooms: Consider formalwear options for yourself and your groomsmen.

❏ Rent any equipment you'll need, such as table, chairs, and tent for an outside wedding.

❏ Finalize your honeymoon arrangements.

❏ Mail out final information on hotel to out-of-town guests.

❏ Decide where you are staying on the night of your wedding and reserve the room.

❏ Work on finding dresses for the moms.

❏ Brides: Give your list of shower guests to your mother, bridesmaids, or whoever else is in charge.

❏ Employ a calligrapher, if you want one.

❏ Choose a baker if necessary; sample and order your wedding cake.

❏ Begin to plan floral selections and discuss prices with your florist.

❏ Finalize wedding insurance, if you have it.

Two to Three Months Before the Wedding

❏ Grooms: Decide on tuxes or suits for you, the groomsmen, and other family members such as the fathers, grandfathers, etc.; if you're renting, have everyone supply their measurements.

❏ Brides: Discuss accessories, jewelry, and shoes with your bridesmaids.

❏ Consider specific items you'll need for your ceremony or reception, such as decorations, an aisle runner, a chuppah, a unity candle holder, and so on.

❏ Brides: Buy any special lingerie you'll need for your dress.

❏ Brides: Confirm delivery of bridal gown and bridesmaids dresses; once they arrive, schedule fittings.

❏ Consult with your families and members of the wedding party about the shower, bachelor/bachelorette parties, etc.

❏ Choose and order your wedding rings.

❏ Purchase or make your wedding favors.

❏ Finalize reception arrangements.

❏ Prepare to get anything you'll need for your honeymoon, such as a passport, birth certificates, vaccinations, and so on.

❏ Pick up your invitations and begin addressing them (or drop them off to the calligrapher).

Six to Eight Weeks Before the Wedding

❏ Mail all invitations to allow time for R.S.V.P.s (if you have many out-of-town guests, give yourself some extra time).

❏ Arrange a time to get your marriage license, and make appointments for your blood tests, if required in your state.

❏ Order liquor, wine, and champagne for your reception, if they aren't included in your contract.

❏ Begin working on your ceremony program.

❏ Start writing your wedding vows, if you're creating your own.

❏ Brides and grooms: make sure you have all of your accessories, if you haven't finalized this already: shoes, jewelry, cufflinks, socks, pocket squares, etc.

❏ Go over parking arrangements, if need be.

❏ Keep a record of gifts as you receive them, and begin to send thank you notes.

❏ Make arrangements for babysitters with your hotel, if necessary.

Three to Four Weeks Before the Wedding

❏ Invite the appropriate people to the rehearsal dinner.

❏ Plan the bridesmaids' luncheon or party, and invite your attendants.

❏ Get your blood tests (if required) and obtain the marriage license.

❏ Confirm that your guests have booked hotel rooms.

❏ Purchase gifts for bridal party and any other important people.

❏ Choose a gift for your fiancé if you will exchange gifts.

❏ Have your final fitting—be sure to remember accessories and shoes.

❏ Schedule appointments at the hair salon for yourself and your attendants.

❏ Choose your makeup and schedule an appointment to get your makeup done, if desired.

❏ Be sure you've finalized and purchased any ceremony and reception accoutrements you'll need, such as a ringbearer's pillow, unity candle holder, champagne flutes, cake cutter, and so on.

❏ Follow up with any guests who haven't responded yet.

❏ Brides: Fill out all the necessary paperwork if changing your name.

❏ Brides: Get your final haircut and have your hairdresser do a test run with your headpiece.

❏ Meet with ceremony musicians and finalize musical selections.

❏ Keep writing thank you notes for all those gifts!

❏ Brides: Practice walking in your shoes; make sure they are comfortable, and break them in.

❏ Finalize readings and other ceremony details with your officiant.

❏ Confirm final headcount and food selections with your reception facility.

❏ Plan ahead for any small tasks you'll need to ask members of the wedding party to do the day of the wedding.

One to Two Weeks Before the Wedding

❏ Finalize your seating arrangements and make your place cards, if your reception site does not provide them.

❏ Prepare newspaper and individual wedding announcements to be mailed after the wedding.

❏ Grooms: Get a haircut.

❏ Shop for any last-minute honeymoon items and start packing.

❏ Pack a separate bag for your wedding night.

❏ Double-check all details with those providing professional services (photographer, videographer, florist, transportation, musicians, etc.); confirm all times and locations.

❏ Write up a short list and confirm desired pictures with photographer; give a copy of the list to someone you trust who can act as a point person for the photographer the day of the wedding.

❏ Practice applying your makeup in proper light.

❏ Grooms: Arrange tux fittings for yourself and others in the wedding; don't leave this until the morning of the wedding!

❏ Finalize specific music selections with DJ/band; arrange for music to start one-half hour prior to ceremony.

❏ Remember to give your families a copy of your honeymoon itinerary.

❏ Make sure the rings fit properly and you have them in a safe place.

❏ Drop off wedding favors, guest book, cake cutter, champagne flutes, and any other things you'll need to your reception site.

❏ Confirm receipt of marriage license.

❏ Organize all of your final cash tips for any vendors/service providers in separate envelopes ahead of time; ask someone you trust to be in charge of giving them out the day of the wedding.

The Day Before the Wedding

❏ Brides: Attend the bridesmaids' luncheon—and enjoy some down-time with your closest girlfriends and family members.

❏ Brides: Get your manicure and pedicure.

❏ Attend rehearsal: Finalize how and when attendants will be walking down the aisle, who will sit where, and so on.

❏ Arrange to have the mother of the groom seated five minutes before ceremony.

❏ Arrange to have the mother of the bride seated immediately before the processional, if she is not walking the bride down the aisle.

❏ Ask two of the groomsmen to roll out the aisle runner immediately before the processional.

❏ Make sure all of your attire and accessories are laid out and ready to go the night before!

❏ Set aside time to spend with just your parents and siblings—this is an exciting but emotional time for everyone, and feelings are bound to be bittersweet.

The Day of the Wedding

❏ Wake up early and give yourself plenty of time to get ready!

❏ Don't forget to eat—you don't want to pass out on the altar.

❏ Bride and Groom: Steal a few private minutes alone together, so you can enjoy your day as a newly married couple.

❏ Thank everyone and tell them how much you love them.

❏ Stay calm, don't stress over small stuff, and enjoy your day!

Scheduling Notes

After the Wedding and Honeymoon

- ❏ Take your gown to be cleaned.
- ❏ Make arrangements for the gifts you've given both sets of parents, to thank them for their help with the wedding.
- ❏ Make sure all vendor bills are completely paid.
- ❏ Get your honeymoon film developed!
- ❏ Freeze the top layer of your wedding cake, so you can enjoy it later.
- ❏ Preserve your bridal bouquet and any other wedding mementos.

Setting Your Date

Now that you've shared your big news, created a smart organizational system, and established a timeline, the next step is arranging your wedding basics. As soon as people hear about your engagement, the first thing you'll hear after "Congratulations!" and "How did he ask you?" is, "When's the date?" Setting the date is the focal point—it will have a direct impact on every last detail of your wedding planning.

What's in a Date?

With 365 days to choose from and a lifetime of married years ahead of you, you've got a lot to think about. Unless you have extenuating circumstances—like a job change that requires you to move to another state—don't be in such a hurry. Don't underestimate the time it takes to plan a wedding. If you plan to have 200 guests and want to pull a big wedding off in six months, that might be a tad unrealistic. On the other hand, some people actually waste more time and find it harder to keep their planning on track when they have an overly long engagement. It's human nature to procrastinate, especially when you know no pressing deadlines are imminent, but slacking off could ultimately put a damper on your big day.

Poised Under Pressure: **Avoid Sensory Overload**

When it comes to wedding-related magazines, books, and Web sites, you can definitely have too much of a good thing. Your best bet is to find one good wedding planning guide (you've already got that in hand), read a few wedding magazines, and register for one Web site, such as www.theknot.com *or* www.weddingchannel.com. *Then cool it. Don't keep buying more magazines or signing up for more Internet advice. It gets too complicated.*

Once you start planning the wedding, sticking to your date will be extremely important as you're dealing with vendors. Many wedding vendors reserve the right to charge a penalty or keep your down payment if you change the date or cancel, and you don't want to lose out.

You probably have all sorts of fantasies floating in your head about what you want your wedding to look and be like, but before you focus on those details, consider these important factors.

- ◆ **Season of choice:** If season doesn't matter to you at all, then you've got all sorts of options. But what if you're thinking country garden wedding in the spring, or maybe a balmy, beachside summer celebration? The season of your celebration will present certain planning issues.

- ◆ **Time constraints:** Remember, small weddings don't require as much work, but large weddings take plenty of time.

- ◆ **Available dates:** If you have a specific ceremony and reception site in mind, do the dates they have available coincide with your desired date? Bear in mind that reception facilities and vendors book up faster and farther in advance in some parts of the country than others.

- ◆ **Prior commitments:** Be mindful of whether any of your family or attendants have other weddings, planned vacations, graduations, pregnancies or births, military commitments, and so on.

◆ **Your budget:** This might be the single largest factor dictating your wedding date. No matter who is contributing financially to the wedding—you and your fiancé, your parents, his parents, or all of the above—a little time might be necessary to save enough money. Coming home from your honeymoon to face wedding debt is no way to start a happy marriage. Budget beforehand!

◆ **Vendor costs:** Because spring and summer weddings are most popular, caterers, photographers, florists, DJs, and bands often boost prices for prime season. In addition, many vendors—reception sites included—will charge more on a Saturday than a Friday. If your budget is tight, these factors can make a big difference on the bottom line.

◆ **Lifestyle:** Depending on your career or lifestyle choices, certain times of the year might work better than others. Planning your wedding for the week after your fiancé takes the bar exam is not the best idea. If he's under that much stress right before the wedding, it's going to put a damper on things!

◆ **Extenuating circumstances:** If the bride is pregnant, for instance, a couple might choose to get married immediately—or wait until after the baby is born. If it's a long-distance relationship, it might be preferable to get married sooner than later. Take those special circumstances into consideration.

Keep in mind that the peak season for weddings is between April and October, so there may be a lot of competition for everything from flowers to frosting in those months. You might find more opportunities if you choose to get married in January, February, or March.

As soon as you've firmed up your wedding date and locked in a ceremony and reception site, start planning the other important elements in your wedding: caterer (if catering isn't provided by your reception site), photographer, videographer, transportation, and music, Flowers, your gown, the bridesmaids' dresses, and other things are also important, but

Classic Concerns: Choosing the Right Vendors

By all means, pick your friends' and family's brains for vendor suggestions. But just because so-and-so took the photos at your cousin's wedding doesn't mean that person is right for you. Have a clear picture of what you need and want from each of your vendors. Be specific and go with those vendors who fit with your vision.

they don't require as much advanced notice as these other linchpins. Remember, starting early will give you the breathing room to take your time and choose wisely.

Choosing a Style

Once you've chosen your wedding date, it's time to flesh out style details. If you're planning to go all out with a themed wedding—Victorian or a Renaissance style, for instance—the style will be dictated by the theme. But if you're having a seasonal event, like a holiday wedding, adding ethnic elements to your wedding, or simply throwing a traditional wedding that incorporates some personal and creative twists, it's helpful to figure out what style you want from the start.

The formality of the event should remain consistent. For instance, you wouldn't want to send formal, engraved invitations to a beach-themed wedding. Likewise, you wouldn't wear a short wedding dress to an elegant, formal evening event. Consistency is what brings everything together; it will help you to pick and choose the right elements when faced with myriad options.

Note: Brides are often unhappy if they feel like everything they must do for their wedding is a chore. If you have a passion, put it to use for your wedding. You're bound to be more upbeat if you weave a favorite hobby, talent, or interest into your wedding plans.

Formal Weddings

Full of high style and glamour, formal weddings are typically quite proper. They follow a somewhat rigid set of guidelines when it comes to attire, invitations, menu, music, and location, although there's room for creativity within those guidelines. The attire is white tie, which means tails, white bow ties, and wing-collared shirts for men. The bride typically wears a dress with a long train and a long veil. Female guests can wear long or short evening dresses, but men should don tuxedos.

Formal weddings are also typically accompanied by upscale, engraved invitations; swank locations, such as an estate, ballroom, or museum; live music; and a sit-down, multicourse meal. They usually involve 200 or more guests.

Semiformal Weddings

Semiformal weddings might have many of the same things—they're just slightly more relaxed. The bride can wear a long or shorter dress, as well as a shorter veil. Bouquets might be simpler and less extravagant. For a semiformal evening wedding, the groom may still wear a tuxedo or a dinner jacket—for daytime, a suit might be more appropriate. Female guests may wear evening dresses or evening suits, while male guests may choose between a tuxedo or a suit.

Semiformal weddings often still include a seated meal, a sizeable wedding party, and live music. But they can also incorporate less formal touches like a DJ, a cocktail reception, or a nice but not-quite-as-formal location, such as a banquet hall or inn.

Informal Weddings

Traditionally, informal weddings have been the style of choice for second weddings, daytime weddings, and theme weddings, including picnic or outdoor weddings. These events are less rigid, with the bride wearing a suit or short dress and the groom in a suit or a classic blazer and trousers. Male and female guests alike should still wear their Sunday best, but it needn't be overly dressy.

With an informal wedding there's a lot more leeway in invitation style, flowers, music, and location. Meals can be less formal, too—buffet or food-station style, or even potluck.

Balancing Tradition with Creativity

As you and your fiancé plan your wedding, you'll get hit with a barrage of traditional elements that might or might not work for you. Your priest, minister, or rabbi will tell you how certain things need to be done, your parents will want you to do things certain ways—heck, even your DJ or videographer might spout preconceived expectations about how your wedding should work. All of these requests and requirements are enough to rattle even the most composed bride-to-be. Do yourself a favor before you lose your cool and examine how you both feel about these demands.

No doubt there are elements of traditional weddings that you inevitably love. Perhaps a certain song sung in church or synagogue holds a special place in your heart, or maybe you tear right up at the thought of dancing with your father. Then there are those traditions that you could take or leave—perhaps the bouquet and garter toss, or the cake cutting. Whether or not you incorporate these traditions is entirely up to you. Just because as a bridesmaid in the past you've been pushed to the front of the group to catch the bouquet, that doesn't mean you have to subject your friends and family to a similar fate.

Classic Concerns: Flexible Formality

Sure, it's wise to remain generally consistent with your wedding planning. But just because you're a "classic" bride, that doesn't mean you have to be rigid. You can break some rules and make adjustments. If you really want a wedding that's informal in most ways, but you also have your sights set on a five-course meal, feel free to do both!

The best way to decide on certain traditions is to ask yourself *why* they should be included. Does a particular element mean something to the two of you, or can you alter it in some way so that it better suits you? Of course, you might want to make some accommodations for the sake of others. For instance, maybe you don't care much about how you get to your ceremony, but your parents have always had their hearts set on riding in a stretch limo with you on your wedding day. Making that adjustment doesn't hurt anything (especially if your parents offer to help defray the cost). But don't be afraid to speak up and eliminate anything you're not comfortable with.

The Wedding Planner

By now, you should have a good idea about what type of wedding you want and what it's going to take to pull it off. Before you sprint out of the starting gate, you should decide if you're comfortable handling all of it on your own, or if you want to enlist a professional planner. Since weddings are their business, good consultants are experienced in every area of wedding planning. They can share access to knowledge, ideas, and contacts you might not otherwise have.

Of course, not everyone needs or wants a consultant. Some brides have plenty of time to plan their wedding. Sure, you're probably not one of them, especially if you're a busy, independent woman with a demanding job and other personal and social commitments to keep with friends and family. But that doesn't mean you can't handle—and enjoy—planning your wedding without a consultant. As long as you hone savvy planning skills and use your time wisely, wedding preparation can be exciting and rewarding. Don't forget that just because you're the bride, that doesn't mean you have to handle everything yourself. Draw on the past experiences of your mother, aunts, sisters, friends, cousins, and leverage the knowledge of your reception site coordinator and vendor—chances are, you'll get some great advice for free.

That said, there are brides who don't have anyone experienced to help them, or feel they don't have the time or energy required to plan the wedding they want. It can be difficult for women who work sixty hours a week and/or happen to live across the country from their mother (or sister, or friends) to plan a wedding by themselves. If this sounds like your life, a consultant might relieve the planning pressure.

Don't fret if, after all is said and done, you don't have room in your budget for a consultant. With any luck, this guide will serve a similar purpose. It might not seem as glamorous or exclusive as working with a private consultant, but it will help you to cut through any wedding-planning confusion so you can plan the wedding of your dreams.

Classic Rewind

You might think you have all the time in the world to plan your wedding, but beware: The last thing you want is to wake up one morning and suddenly realize that it's a month before your wedding, yet your gown still hasn't arrived because you ordered it too late. Once you plan your schedule, stick to it. Think of it this way: If you accomplish all that you can up front, later on, you'll stay calm because last-minute details won't throw you. Keep your eye on that prize, and when your wedding day finally rolls around, you'll be relaxed and ready to wow everyone.

Extra Notes

Extra Notes

Extra Notes

Extra Notes

Extra Notes

Extra Notes

Extra Notes

Extra Notes

Extra Notes

Extra Notes

Extra Notes

Budget Concerns

In This Section:

Intro to Budgeting

Intro to Budgeting

Welcome to a beginner's course on budgeting: How much do you have, how much are you willing to part with, and who's paying for what? These "uncivilized" details will have quite an impact on your wedding!

*Y*our budget (if you stick to it) will dictate the size and overall style of your wedding, as well as all the other individual details, such as flowers, music, photography, videography, and transportation. If you're a busy bride, you won't have time to waste dealing with the stress of poor budget planning, and you certainly won't want to face the challenge of cutting or revising your budget later in the game. Set the right budget now so you can follow through with all your planning.

As soon as you decide on the type of wedding you want, shape a budget that hits the mark as closely as possible, without going for broke. Maybe you and your fiancé don't even want a "big" formal (or semiformal) wedding. If you both shy away from frills and thrills, you might prefer a small, simple affair. But what if you want to have as many of the things that go along with a grand wedding as your budget will allow? In either case, planning your expenses wisely is important, so you can stretch every dollar.

Get Ready to Pay—a Lot

When planning your budget, it's always best to be prepared for whatever might come your way. No matter what you *expect* to spend, more expenses always sneak in. Remember, finances are often a stumbling block in relationships, and the engagement period is no exception. You and your fiancé might find yourselves duking it out in this department. Keep money matters in perspective from the start, and you won't have a meltdown when things get complicated later on.

Most all weddings are expensive these days, but everyone's idea of expense varies—especially by region. A nice, average wedding in the Northeast is bound to cost you a fortune more than one in the certain parts of the Midwest. Formality levels vary by region, too. While an informal backyard buffet reception might be common in some areas, it's typically not the norm in others, where more formal reception facilities are often employed. You and your fiancé will need to discuss your individual expectations—and you'll have

Poised Under Pressure: **Borrow a Budget**

The less concrete your ideas about wedding costs, the more conflicts you and your fiancé are bound to have over money. So don't just ask other newlywed family members and friends for vague ballpark figures. Shoot for specific breakdowns. Though your figures might differ from theirs in the end, at least you'll be better prepared when hit with each cost.

to do your homework. If you have friends or relatives who've recently been married, you're sitting pretty, because they'll be a tremendous resource to you in the budget department. Don't be shy about asking them how much they paid for particular services. Having survived the struggles themselves, most newlyweds are happy to pass on the wisdom they've gained.

According to estimates from *Brides* magazine and *Wedding* magazine, in 2003, the average wedding in the United States with 150 to 200 guests cost anywhere between $20,000 to $28,000—18 percent more than four years prior. Now consider that these estimates don't include the honeymoon, and that estimates for costs in the Northeast can skew as high as $35,000 to $45,000+. It's enough to make you want to find the nearest ladder, sneak off, and elope. There are ways to make it work, however, and good budgeting is the key.

Budget Basics

The dictionary defines the word budget as follows: "An itemized summary of estimated or intended expenditures for a given period along with proposals for financing them." (*American Heritage Dictionary of the English Language, Fourth Edition.*) That last part's the clincher. You can daydream all you want about the fab fête Brad and Jen had, but if your wallet's telling you otherwise, it's time to come back down to Earth and create a *viable* plan. (Remember, their marriage went bust, and that's exactly what will happen to your budget if you're not careful!)

Perhaps you already keep a monthly budget, planning for living expenses and also budgeting for the unexpected, like car repairs—or that great pair of shoes that goes on sale for half price. A wedding budget is similar—it's a plan that accounts for expected and unexpected expenditures. If you've always been rather vague when it comes to budgeting, settling money matters for your wedding will be your financial wakeup call. But even if you're accustomed to accounting for everything you spend, you've probably never had to balance a budget of this scale! Either way, planning your wedding budget just might be the start of a new way of looking at how you spend.

Poised Under Pressure: **Making Compromises**

If you're one of the lucky few who has the funds available to finance the wedding of your dreams, congratulations! In reality, most couples find themselves a few dollars short of their dream. Don't despair! Savvy brides learn where and how to make compromises and cuts that will save them a bundle of cash without detracting from the overall outcome of their wedding. You'll find plenty of these suggestions throughout this planner.

Budget Pop Quiz

Knowing what each one of you wants is the first step to planning your wedding. Grab your fiancé and take this easy quiz together. It will help you lay some groundwork for your budget.

1. Where do you want to have your wedding ceremony and reception?
2. How many people will you invite?
3. How much can you spend on the wedding and reception?
4. Who will pay for the wedding and reception?
5. If the two of you will pay for all or part of the wedding, how will you finance it?
6. Where will you go on your honeymoon, and how much will you spend?

Your Answers

Were your ideas and dreams for your wedding alike, or were they miles apart? Perhaps one of you wants to have a big fancy wedding and has no reservations about using your credit card when money runs out, and the idea is enough to make the other faint.

Don't worry—even the most compatible couples can have varying visions of their wedding day. Whether you have different expectations based on the wedding you've always imagined and the kinds of weddings that are customary in each of your families, or different priorities because of your plans for the future, be prepared for wedding planning to require communication and compromise.

Once you create a budget, you'll be able to prioritize what's most important to you. Then you can find ways to save money on certain items or services that don't matter as much, and put that extra money toward the things that are more significant.

First Things First: Priorities

Ultimately, you'll need to prioritize different elements of your wedding so you can allocate finances properly. Keep in mind that although certain extras are nice, you and your guests won't necessarily miss them because they don't have a huge impact on the overall quality of your wedding. Other things, however, will live on in your memory long after the actual day has passed. Those are the important things that you'll carry with you into your future.

Start by asking yourselves which wedding elements are important to you. Each of you should make a list, and then star two or three top things. Then you'll know how and where you'll want to focus money and time within your budget.

For example, if you have a fabulous idea for a three-dimensional invitation that you know will cost more than a traditional flat invitation, you might skip a professional wedding program and make one yourself. Prioritizing is the first commonsense way to achieve your goals on a limited budget.

Who Pays for What?

Traditionally, the bride's family bore the brunt of the wedding expenses and the groom's family picked up the tab for a few select things, but this is changing. In the past, there's been all sorts of etiquette detailing which side of the family pays for what, as in: Bride's family pays for the reception, flowers, invitations, and announcements; groom's family pays for the rehearsal dinner, officiant's fee, and marriage license, and so on. If you are bent on following tradition to the T, that's fine. Otherwise, spare yourself those exacting details, and simply do what works for everyone involved.

Since nowadays a lot of couples are older when they get married, many are more financially secure than couples in the past, so they can pay for their own wedding. The thought of shelling out all this money for one single day might very well freak you out—especially once you begin to discover how much each component will cost. Just keep in mind that your own opinions carry more weight if *you* are the one writing the check.

If you and your fiancé will be paying for some or all of your wedding, determine how you'll make it work as soon as possible. Will you set up a joint account just for the wedding (this is a good idea), or will you make the payments and deposits as needed and divide them? Making this determination sooner rather than later will help you to feel calmer and more confident about your financial situation.

The Hidden Costs

Remember that when others are helping to foot the bill, they might feel they have a say about how the money is spent. Your parents will probably expect you to consider their suggestions carefully. You and your fiancé will have to consider the "hidden costs" of accepting money if you feel there might be problems. Your wedding—and planning it—is supposed to be a joyous occasion, not one fraught with controversy and conflict.

Classic Concerns: Ask for Discounts

Most people know about discounts for senior citizens, but there are often other discounts available for students, those who work for certain businesses and professions, AAA members, repeat customers, and so on. Make sure you check into these options before accepting a price.

Poised Under Pressure: **A Set Number of Guests**

Be as specific as possible about the number of guests you're inviting from the start. Depending on where you have your wedding, adding an extra twenty or thirty people to your list could add hundreds—or thousands—of dollars to your costs.

How Big Is Your Budget?

Decide how much you can comfortably spend, then build yourself a cushion, in case you need to stretch your basic budget if you discover something unexpected you want or need for your wedding. Given your own ideas of how much money is "a lot," as well as what you've read in magazines or heard from family and friends, determine whether your budget will be modest, moderate, or luxurious.

Escaping the Perilous Money Pit

While money is unarguably the biggest source of disagreement between married couples, the real issue is not how much money you have, but the way you reach an agreement on how you will spend it. Making your financial decisions—for the wedding and for life—through discussion, compromise, and sound budgeting principles will set the stage for success. Put the following principles to work when planning your wedding expenses, and continue to apply them to other financial situations in the future.

Spending Style

Does a stressful day at the office drive you to a frivolous spending spree at the mall? Or do you find it hard to spend money, and give every potential purchase so much thought others squirm when shopping with you?

Neither extreme is good; if one of you is an impulsive spender and the other is painfully frugal, this combination can spell disaster for financial decisions you make as a couple.

Your Attitudes About Spending

Your attitudes about spending are determined by what you observed growing up. If there were fights over money in your family, you might believe that certain spending styles are bad. Your childhood experiences will lead you to make financial decisions accordingly, and you might be critical of others who have different spending styles. Maybe there were no fights over money in your family (if so, that's amazing!). In that case, with any luck, you've developed a healthy attitude about money, and you'll carry that into your own marriage.

Cash, Check, or Charge?

Once you set the wheels in motion, get ready to pay dearly—and quickly—because there are no grace periods when it comes to paying for a wedding. You'll have to dig out your wallet the minute you sign the reception contract and hire your first vendor, because most everyone requires a deposit. You have three choices: cash, check, or charge. Since most people don't walk around with wads of money on hand, this discussion will stick to the check and charge options.

Cash on Reserve

If either set of parents has set aside a lump sum for the wedding, you can do one of three things. Ask your parents to deposit the money into an account so you can write checks as necessary; have your parents send the checks directly to the person or place being hired (keep in mind that if someone else's check gets there first, they might beat you to it); or, set up a separate checking account just for the wedding money.

Classic Concerns: Savvy Spending

As mentioned earlier in this book, always remember to get everything in writing. You're spending enough on your wedding—you don't want to shell out additional payments when you find that your arrangements have fallen through. Verbal assurances are never enough—there's too much at stake!

This last option might prove the easiest. For one thing, you know that the money you set aside in this account is solely for wedding expenses, and you're not accidentally tapping into your rent money. You'll also have your cancelled checks as proof that your deposits and payments were cashed—just in case a question arises.

Credit Card Pros and Cons

It's best to put big purchases on a credit card. You'll have more consumer recourse if something goes wrong. You might also reap the benefits of points, air miles, or other promotional programs. Your honeymoon is the perfect opportunity to take advantage of such perks, so call your credit card company and see what's available. Be sure to read the terms and conditions closely. If you're a disciplined spender, using a credit card can be a handy way of keeping track of your deposits and payments. Just be careful to keep close tabs on how much you charge each month so you're not surprised when your statement arrives.

A word of warning: Don't think of your credit card as a one-way ticket to anything and everything you want for your wedding. Spend only what you're sure you can pay for, and pay off each bill as it comes in so you don't accrue unnecessary interest or damage your credit rating. (No bank is going to care about that perfect dress you just *had* to have when it comes time to apply for a mortgage!)

Projected Costs

Regardless of whether you are planning a modest, moderate, or luxurious wedding, you'll need to account for the basics and allocate particular amounts of money for particular items and services. Typically, the two most important factors that influence wedding expenditures are size and location. Since the bill for the reception often eats up as much as one-half of a wedding's total budget, establishing the number of guests is crucial. Wedding and reception venues vary widely in price. Each facility offers a different package—some include hors d'oeuvres and open bar, while others provide just the basic meal and charge an à la carte fee for additional services.

After you've considered the above, establish ballpark estimates for other wedding expenses. Consult with family and friends, then pick up the phone and start dialing. Call a variety of reception sites and caterers, and ask for their wedding menus to get an idea of how much per-person charges can run. Figure in tax, and ask about additional fees, such as rental, setup, gratuity, or corkage fees. Do the same with photographers, limousine services, videographers, and any other services.

When you have specifics in hand, weigh up the cost ranges. This will help you to prioritize which things are most important.

Poised Under Pressure: **Curb Spending Sprees**

It's easy to get caught up in the excitement of planning a wedding. Resist the urge to snap up anything and everything in sight, however. Before making purchases for your wedding—especially the big-ticket items like a wedding dress—think carefully about why you need or want the item. Mull things over, wait to see how you feel the next day, and then make your decision.

Some costs are fully within your control. For instance, you might read in a magazine that the average cost of a wedding gown is $1,000, or that the average amount spent on wedding favors is $250 to $300, and then decide to stay within those limits. But what if you read that the average price for a reception with 150 to 200 guests is $6,000 to $8,000, and then find out that the going rate is at least double in your state? That's why it's best to do your own research first and interview several vendors and reception locations before making your final decision.

Your Budget in Black and White

The following list should help you to assess your budget needs and break down your costs. Once you review this worksheet, start a computerized spreadsheet that will keep track of your finances for you, so you'll know exactly what you've paid, and when.

For each item, be sure to create columns for projected cost, including tax, any deposits you pay, remaining balances due, and who is paying.

Wedding Budget Worksheet

Wedding Consultant

Fee _____

Tip (usually 15–20 percent) _____

Prewedding Parties

*Engagement Party*_____

Site rental _____

Equipment rental _____

Invitations _____

Food _____

Beverages _____

Decorations _____

Flowers _____

Party favors _____

Bridesmaids' Party/Luncheon _____

Rehearsal Dinner _____

Site rental _____

Equipment rental _____

Invitations _____

Food _____

Beverages _____

Decorations _____

Flowers _____

Party favors _____

Additional Wedding Weekend Parties _____

Ceremony

Location fee _____

Officiant's fee _____

Donation to church (optional, amount varies) _____

Organist _____

Vocalist _____

Other musicians _____

Tips (amounts vary) _____

Programs _____

Aisle runner _____

Reception

Site rental _____

Equipment rental (chairs, tent, etc.) _____

Decorations _____

Servers, bartenders _____

Beer, wine, liquor _____

Nonalcoholic beverages _____

Hors d'oeuvres _____

Entrees _____

Wedding cake/dessert _____

Meals for vendors/hired help _____

Toasting glasses _____

Cake serving set and decorations _____

Guest book and pen _____

Favors _____

Box/basket for envelope gifts _____

Tip for caterer or banquet manager (usually 15–20 percent) _____

Tip for servers, bartenders (usually 15–20 percent) _____

Legal Matters

Marriage license _____

Blood test (if applicable) _____

Bride's Attire

Wedding gown _____

Alterations _____

Undergarments (slip, bustier, hosiery, etc.) _____

Veil/headpiece _____

Shoes _____

Purse _____

Makeup _____

Hair _____

Going away outfit _____

Honeymoon clothes _____

Groom's Attire

Tuxedo _____

Shoes _____

Going away outfit _____

Honeymoon clothes _____

Wedding Jewelry

Bride's wedding band _____

Groom's wedding band _____

Additional jewelry (necklace, earrings, cufflinks, etc.) _____

Gifts

Bride's attendants _____

Groom's attendants _____

Other ceremony participants (readers, for instance) _____

Parents _____

Bride (optional) _____

Groom (optional) _____

Photography/Videography

Engagement portrait _____

Wedding portrait _____

Photographer's fee _____

Wedding proofs _____

Album _____

Parents' albums _____

Extra prints _____

Videographer's fee _____

Extra videos/DVDs _____

Reception Music

Musicians for cocktail hour _____

Live Band/DJ _____

Tips (15–20 percent) _____

Flowers and Decorations

Flowers for wedding site _____

Decorations for wedding site _____

Bride's bouquet _____

Bridesmaids' flowers _____

Boutonnieres _____

Corsages _____

Flowers for reception site _____

Table centerpieces _____

Classic Concerns: Your Honeymoon Budget

Don't forget to figure your honeymoon into the overall budget. It's easy to push that aside and think of it as separate from your actual wedding budget. But this money's not going to appear magically for you right before your wedding; you've got to plan for it to come from somewhere.

Flowers for the cake/cake table _____

Decorations for reception _____

Wedding Invitations and Stationery

Invitations _____

Announcements _____

Thank-you notes _____

Calligrapher _____

Postage _____

Transportation

Limousines or rented cars _____

Parking _____

Tips for drivers _____

Additional guest transportation _____

Honeymoon
. . . .

Transportation _____

Accommodations _____

Meals _____

Spending money _____

Additional Miscellaneous Expenses _____
. . . .

Grand Total _____
. . . .

This is the *long* list. Obviously, not every one of these items will apply to you. For starters, if you have a reception facility that charges you per plate, things like tax and tips for the servers and wait staff are probably calculated up front. You also won't have to worry about renting equipment or tents. Further, there's no rule that says you must sit for a formal engagement or wedding portrait, employ a calligrapher, or enlist the services of strolling musicians for your cocktail hour! All of these items are simply included to give you an idea of your options.

Classic Rewind

Estimates vary, but between one-third and one-half of couples pay for their wedding themselves. Whether you're lucky enough to have families who can foot the bill, or you're paying for some or all of your wedding on your own, this is probably the most expensive affair you've ever planned. That overwhelming sense of responsibility can complicate the decision-making process. If you set a workable budget and then bring your wedding expenses in line with that financial plan, you'll be better equipped to make decisions and you'll feel great about everything once your wedding day arrives. You'll also have sharpened your financial planning skills for the future.

Budgeting Notes

Preparing for the Unexpected

When you budget for the unexpected, you have to be prepared to handle *anything*. That's why you need that spot in your budget for "miscellaneous" expenses. This one small column can and probably will encompass many things. Think of this as the spot that covers all those extras you never realized you had to budget for—the things that come at you out of the blue once your wedding planning is underway.

You might reserve as little as 2 percent or as much as 10 percent or more of your budget for miscellaneous expenses, depending on what you consider "miscellaneous." Many couples don't give miscellaneous expenses a second thought—until they add things up and realize that 5 percent of a $20,000 total wedding budget is a hefty $1,000. Some brides and grooms forget to figure in the cost of essential items like the marriage license. Others fail to calculate a realistic cost for favors, disregard tips and gratuities, or neglect the cost of invitation postage. That's why it's best to be as specific as possible in your budget breakdowns.

And yet, we all know that old saying about even the best-laid plans going awry. As you get closer to your wedding day, you'll probably end up purchasing all sorts of incidentals—Band-Aids or first-aid supplies, extra pantyhose . . . Be prepared, because these incidentals add up!

An Unexpected Turn of Events

Sometimes you can unexpectedly blow your budget when you're forced to change plans at the last minute. For example, if you're having an outdoor wedding, you'll have to be prepared to provide an alternate solution in case of rain, and this could involve substantial costs. Some couples buy a large number of umbrellas to keep on hand, or rent a tent, and then realize they didn't include these costs in their original estimates. Suddenly there's a blip in the miscellaneous category, and the money's got to come from somewhere. Make sure you're covered for these things.

Classic Concerns: **What Miscellaneous Means**

Everyone has different ideas about what constitutes a valid miscellaneous expense. If one of you thinks it's no big deal to spend a few extra dollars for the shoes you really want or the perfect veil you just saw, but the other does, you've got a problem on your hands that needs to be discussed.

Time to Borrow?

There are times when, despite your best efforts, the money simply runs out. Maybe you underestimated your expenses. Perhaps that money you expected to receive from parents or relatives isn't forthcoming, or that CD you counted on comes with a hefty penalty for early withdrawal. No one thinks it's a good idea to borrow a lot of money or rack up lots of credit card debt to pay for a wedding. That said, if what you have is a temporary situation and you don't want to borrow much, you might consider a loan.

Keep It in the Family

Turning to family first is usually the best idea, unless those are the same people who caused the problem to begin with by reneging on their offer to help financially. Your family will most likely give you a break, and these sorts of loans don't require credit approval or accrue interest charges. If you feel uncomfortable about asking for a loan from your family, draw up and sign a note for the money, with the terms for repayment stated clearly. Make it clear that you intend to honor your commitment, not treat the money like a gift.

Turn to a Financial Institution

If you have to borrow money from a financial institution, try to take out a loan using your savings or CD account as collateral (which will stay in the bank or credit union until the loan is repaid, or as parts of it are repaid). If you don't have a savings account, a local bank or credit union might still approve a loan.

As much as possible, avoid overcharging your credit cards. However, when all else fails, use a credit card with the lowest interest first. Remember to check out whether taking out a cash advance carries a lower interest rate. Some credit cards offer introductory 0 percent interest rates for a certain period of time. This might be a realistic option if you know you can pay off the debt within the allotted time frame.

Tipping the Scales

There are lots of budget-breakers out there, but tipping is one substantial expense that even the most budget-conscious brides and grooms often overlook. Depending on the size of your reception and your reception location, tipping can easily add a few hundred to a few thousand dollars to your costs. Many wedding professionals even include a gratuity in their contract, and then expect an additional tip at the reception.

Who to tip and how much to give them can often be perplexing dilemmas. If you're employing separate individuals to provide bar service, food service, and so on, work out separate tipping arrangements. If all services are included in your reception contract, discuss these specifics with your facility's reception coordinator in advance.

If your wedding day flows flawlessly, you'll have lots of people to thank, including caterers, the reception facility's host or hostess, wait staff, bartenders, delivery people, the photographer, the videographer, musicians, limo drivers . . . . All of that appreciation can add up fast. Be prepared to add enough money for tips into your budget. Although tipping is, for the most part, expected, it is never required—it is simply an extra reward for extraordinary service. Use your discretion.

When Vendors and Venues Let You Down

What do you do when the bakery that was supposed to bake your wedding cake goes out of business, your wedding dress arrives without the matching chiffon shawl you ordered, or your reception site accidentally double-books your banquet room, leaving you high and dry?

First, check your contract. Most contracts should allow for unforeseen circumstances. For example, if your DJ or one of the members in your band gets sick, they should be prepared to make arrangements for a replacement at a moment's notice. Consider what provisions you've made for deposits to be returned. If this leads you nowhere, the next step is nicely but firmly threatening to contact the Better Business Bureau. Write letters, and don't back off. Make yourself a thorn in this individual's side, so they know they can't walk away from the mess.

If you've got an even bigger problem on your hands—let's say you've made a large deposit on a reception site and now, after double-booking, the facility refuses to come up with a workable compromise—contact an attorney. Most attorneys will be able to resolve problems without expensive litigation and court appearances in civil actions.

Classic Concerns: Be Smart about Saving Money

If you've always found haggling distasteful, now might be the time to sharpen those skills. Vendor fees can be negotiable—often, vendors would rather compromise on a price than lose the sale. For example, ask your florist if you can get a discount for placing the order and putting down a deposit six months in advance. Or, offer to have a friend pick up the cake to save on a delivery fee.

What about Wedding Insurance?

You probably don't even want to think about it, but it has to be said. Your wedding is one of the biggest investments you will ever make; many couples spend more on their wedding than they would for an automobile or a trip abroad. Logically then, wedding insurance might be a good idea.

True, if you've been charging everything on a credit card, you should have backup in case anything happens. Hopefully, you've been cautious about signing all of your contracts and putting every detail pertaining to goods and services in writing—and that's great. However, those steps might not get your money back if something unforeseen happens.

If you're having your wedding and reception at a private home, you might want to get insurance in case someone is injured or there is damage to property (the homeowner's insurance policy may cover it if you choose not to buy wedding insurance). Did you know that some reception sites require you to carry wedding insurance? Weigh all of these options, and consider adding wedding insurance costs into your budget if necessary.

Contact your insurance agent for quotes, or research wedding insurance companies on the Internet. Costs vary. You'll have to decide if it's worth the extra money (possibly a few hundred dollars for a wedding in the five figures), and you'll need to include the cost in your budget to protect your investment.

Classic Concerns: Track Your Spending

Consistent bookkeeping is the best way to lighten the burden of miscellaneous expenses. Be faithful about recording even those expenses that seem small. Ten dollars here and there might not seem like a lot, but over the course of a few months, those small expenditures add up. Don't wait until this happens and you're in jeopardy of not having enough money in your account to pay for something really important. Keep track of everything you spend.

Classic Rewind

Think of your wedding budget as one of the first places that you and your fiancé hash out your attitudes about money, juggle specific expenditures, cope with financial challenges, and work together to plan your marriage. It's the perfect time to establish constructive methods for dealing with the unforeseen setbacks that will inevitably arise throughout your marriage. Even if one of you is doing most of the planning and spending, it's important that you both agree on how this will be done. That spirit of budgetary responsibility will foster a sense of teamwork and marital harmony.

Any financial challenges you face for your wedding will teach you to work together as a team. It's great practice for the Real Thing—life as a married couple—and that's worth everything: trials, tribulations, and heated discussions included.

Extra Notes

Extra Notes

Extra Notes

Extra Notes

Extra Notes

Extra Notes

Extra Notes

Ceremony Chic

Ceremony Chic

Chapter Three

Ceremonial Savvy

Time to plan your ceremony! You've got to a lot to do, from finding a location to choosing music and writing your own vows. But before you do that, you need to decide on who will be standing at your sides during the ceremony.

Assembling Your Wedding Party

ome brides-to-be have had a crystal clear idea of who they want standing beside them as they make their commitment to married life. For others whose options are too numerous to negotiate easily—sisters, cousins, childhood companions, high-school pals, college roommates—this selection process poses more of a dilemma. On top of that, there are the groom's VIPs to figure into the mix, and suddenly, choosing the wedding party becomes quite a process. Don't let this stress you out. These people are supposed to be there to support you during your wedding planning, not add angst to your life! The fact is, you'll have to narrow it down—you'll never be able to choose every single one of your cousins or all ten of your freshman-year floormates. You're having a wedding, not a three-ring circus—good taste and discretion should rule.

Follow your instincts, and choose the people you and your fiancé feel most comfortable with. Having the right group of people in your wedding party will ensure you'll be surrounded by the right amount of support, comfort, and laughter during those occasionally trying times.

Also remember that there are many other parts to be played in the course of a wedding besides being a bridesmaid or groomsman. Choose special people to do a reading or hand out programs at your ceremony. If you have any singers or musicians in your circle of family and friends, ask them to do that honor. At a Catholic wedding, gift bearers play an important role, as do those who sign the Ketubah (marriage contract) and hold the Chuppah (wedding canopy) at Jewish ceremonies.

The Numbers Game

Your wedding party can be as big—or as small—as you like. Formal weddings usually have more attendants than informal ones, but feel free to bend tradition.

Brides often feel obligated to have certain people in their wedding. Don't feel pressured into choosing attendants because of what others will think, what your parents want, or what will make somebody else happy.

Poised Under Pressure: **Connected Wedding Party**

As soon as possible, send out a list to everyone with the names, addresses, phone numbers, and e-mails of each member of your wedding party. This way, you can take yourself out of the equation when you don't need to be involved, and things will run more smoothly!

Poised Under Pressure: **Odd Man Out?**

Don't agonize over it if your fiancé has one person more or less in the wedding party than you, it's perfectly acceptable. Your wedding isn't about perfect symmetry; it's about including the people who truly matter to you.

Once you see how smoothly all those prewedding parties, fittings, and rehearsals will go and how much fun you'll have with the right mix of people in your wedding party, you'll be glad you decided to choose your closest friends and family members—the ones you know you can depend on.

Double Wedding Duty

Don't fret if you've set a date, and shortly after, one of your bridesmaids gets engaged, too. Planning a wedding at the same time as another close friend or family member can be a lot of fun. With a little juggling, some solid planning, and support from others, things will work out just fine. And, in years to come, you'll be glad the two of you were able to share the special, once-in-a-lifetime experience together.

The To-Do Lists

As soon as you and your fiancé figure out who you want in your wedding party, get on out there and ask them. Now for some good news—here's a rundown of tasks typically performed by each member of the wedding party. Remember, though, none of these rules are set in stone.

The maid/matron of honor:

- ◆ Organizes the bridal shower (often along with the bride's mother).
- ◆ Fixes the bride's train and veil during the ceremony.
- ◆ Brings the groom's ring to the ceremony site.

- Holds the bride's bouquet while she exchanges rings with the groom.
- Signs the wedding certificate as a witness.
- Gives a toast at the reception (if she wants).
- Helps the bride primp for pictures.
- Dances with the best man during the attendants' dance.
- Possibly takes charge of the wedding gown after the wedding.

Then, there are other responsibilities that the maid/matron of honor and bridesmaids share:

- Assist the bride with prewedding errands and tasks.
- Help to plan, organize, and run the bridal shower.
- Stand in the receiving line (optional).
- Help the bride get dressed and ready on the wedding day.
- Pose for pictures before and after the ceremony.
- Supply guests with the proper paraphernalia if bubbles or birdseed will be used outside after the ceremony.
- Help out whenever the bride's in need of moral support or assistance!

The best man:

- Organizes the bachelor party. (This is what really matters to the groom; if you're the bride, on the other hand, you might not be so amused!)
- Drives the groom to the ceremony.
- Brings the bride's ring to the ceremony site.
- Gives the officiant his fee immediately before or after the ceremony (this fee is often provided by either set of parents).
- Gives other service providers, such as the chauffeur, their fees and tips. (Your groom, or one of the parents should be in charge of giving the best man the appropriate amounts ahead of time.)

- Returns the groom's attire (if rented).
- Oversees the transfer of gifts to a secure location after reception.
- Helps the groom get ready and arrive on time for the wedding.
- Holds the bride's ring during the ceremony.
- Signs the wedding certificate.
- Escorts the maid of honor in the recessional.
- Poses for pictures with the groom and the wedding party.
- Dances with the maid of honor during the attendants' dance.
- Gives the first toast at the reception.
- May drive the couple to the reception and/or the hotel afterward.

The groomsmen/ushers:

- Arrive at the wedding location early to help with setup.
- Attend to last-minute tasks such as lighting candles, tying bows on reserved rows of seating, and so on.
- Roll out the aisle runner immediately before the processional.
- Escort guests to their seats.
- Seat the eldest guests first if a large group arrives.
- Show guests of honor, such as the grandparents, to their specially assigned seats.

Poised Under Pressure: **Advance Notice**

Give your attendants ample time to plan and save for your wedding. Six months is the absolute minimum. You're not only doing them a favor, you're helping yourself, too. You won't feel so rushed or pressured with your attendants standing by, ready to help.

- Escort female guests with right arm as her escort follows, or lead a couple to their seat.
- Collect discarded programs and articles from pews after ceremony.
- Direct guests to reception as needed.
- Assist in gathering the wedding party for photographs.
- Decorate the getaway vehicle. (If the groomsmen are real pranksters, you might want to keep an eye on this, too!)
- Help out when the groom is in need of moral support or assistance!

Special Considerations

Obviously, planning a wedding isn't a walk in the park. You need help, and that's one reason you're choosing certain people as your attendants. But what if your best friend lives overseas? Or what if your closest friend is a man? How can you include these people, and what should you expect of them?

LONG-DISTANCE MAID OF HONOR

The maid of honor has considerable responsibility before the wedding. Keep in mind that an out-of-town maid of honor can't be expected to help with as much of the planning as someone who lives locally. That said, if you plan carefully, you can figure out ways for her to be helpful without being in the same time zone. Talk to her as soon as possible about what she can do from afar.

Classic Concerns: **Decisions, Decisions**

Nothing says that if you have more than one sister or two best friends, they both can't share the maid-of-honor role. Two honor attendants might add up to twice the help.

Classic Concerns: Expectant Bridesmaids

What if you have pregnant bridesmaids? Don't worry—many designers now offer maternity-style bridesmaids' dresses. Just make allowances for the other, nonpregnant maids to wear something different—they won't want to wear tents!

Your Best Guy Pal

What about a really close guy friend? There's no reason why he shouldn't be included in your wedding party. And don't automatically assume your honor attendant has to be female, either. If you have only one brother, for example, and the two of you are extremely close, why not make him your man of honor or honor attendant? Just because a guy doesn't wear a dress or dance with an usher, that doesn't mean he can't support you in many of the ways a bridesmaid or maid of honor would. Heck, really brave male attendants have even been known to pitch in on traditionally "feminine" duties, such as planning the bridal shower, shopping for the wedding gown, and arranging the bride's train and veil at the altar.

If a guy is taking the place of your maid of honor, he can stand on your side during the ceremony, and in the processional and recessional he can walk in after the rest of the bride's attendants. Or, if there are more brides-maids than ushers, he can escort one of the bridesmaids.

Likewise, there's nothing wrong with your fiancé choosing a best woman. It's also perfectly acceptable to have female ushers at your wed-ding, providing the females in question are comfortable with the idea. These women attendants can either wear the same dress as the brides-maids, or wear something different that coordinates with the rest of the wedding party.

> ### *Poised Under Pressure:* Think Twice About Kids
>
> *Little kids can be unpredictable, so you might want to avoid having chil-dren under five in your wedding. And if you simply have too many little cousins or nieces and nephews from which to choose, save on stress and cut out kids in the ceremony altogether.*

Kids' Stuff

If you or your fiancé have younger relatives (or children of your own), you might want to make them part of your ceremony. Girls between ten and fourteen are usually junior bridesmaids; flower girls are younger. Little boys, usually under ten, can be ringbearers.

The ringbearer usually precedes the flower girl in the procession. (The flower girl is the last person down the aisle before the bride.) If you've got a shy ringbearer or flower girl, the kids can totter down the aisle side-by-side, or if you're really patient, you might ask one of their parents to coax them down toward their final destination. The ringbearer carries a satin pillow, and the rings are usually attached with a ribbon. Good news for the faint of heart: The rings this little guy carries are fake, so you don't have to worry if he loses them. Remember, the best man and/or maid of honor hold onto the real rings. Other little boys and girls, called trainbearers or pages, can follow behind the bride, carrying her train, and then arranging it neatly.

The Parents' Part

Just a minute . . . before you put all the wedding party considerations behind you—you're not done yet. Last, but certainly not least, both sets of parents are integral parts of the wedding party. Your parents do much more than simply sign the checks. Keep in mind that this is a special day in their lives, too. They get to dress the part and even chime in with their opinions once in a while.

Your Parents

Your dad might not seem to take as much interest in the day-to-day wedding planning the way your mom probably will. On the surface, it might seem like it's your father's job to just accompany you to the church, walk you down the aisle, and give you away. In reality, his more important (and unspoken) responsibilities usually involve fretting about how he's going to pay for the wedding, and being sad that his little girl has grown up and he now has to share her with another important man in her life. While it's easy to get caught up in all of the "girlie" stuff as you search with your mom and bridesmaids for dresses, veils, shoes, and such, don't neglect your dad. Keep him in the loop about things, ask him to help in whatever ways he likes, and give him a little extra TLC, too.

Your father gets his moment in the sun when he walks you down the aisle and shares that special dance with you at the reception. Shouldn't the woman who endured hours of labor to give you life be included as well? At the onset of the ceremony, the mother is the last person seated before the processional begins. But, like your attendants, she has plenty to do before the wedding, both officially and unofficially.

The mother of the bride:

- Helps her daughter with the search for the perfect wedding gown and accessories.
- Offers advice on bridesmaids dresses.
- Works with her daughter and the groom's family to assemble a guest list and seating plan.
- Coordinates the bridal shower with the attendants.
- Helps address and mail invitations.
- Occupies a place of honor at the ceremony and at the parents' table during the reception.
- Stands at the beginning of the receiving line.
- May act as hostess during the reception.

Beyond these things, however, her biggest official duty is to lend moral support and assist with all the details. She'll patiently sympathize as you complain about *not* being able to find that "perfect" gown, and she'll calm your dad as he ponders how he's going to avoid bankruptcy once this wedding is over. Your mother will also most likely bear the brunt of your random emotional outbursts and unnecessary verbal assaults whenever you're behaving badly because of wedding-planning anxiety. You'll probably feel the need to argue with her *a lot* during this time. If you're lucky enough to have a mom who's a real angel through it all, thank your lucky stars, and remember to sing her praises.

His Parents

These people have a pretty easy time of it, in comparison to the duties that are heaped on your mom and dad. As they sit at the parents' table during the reception and have their picture taken all day long, they'll probably be thinking about how lucky they are to have a son, so they didn't get stuck with all that planning and financial expense. *Unless* you're lucky (and smart) enough to convince your in-laws to divide the wedding duties (and/or finances) equally with your parents.

Classic Rewind

When choosing your wedding party, pick people who are comfortable working with others, who don't get flustered easily, and who have known you or your groom for a long time. Your wedding is no time for surprises. Also don't be afraid to make nontraditional, unusual choices when assembling your wedding party. Some of the most memorable weddings include unexpected, personal choices that break the traditional rules. Whatever you decide, don't waste time second guessing yourself—most people will understand and respect your choices, and if they don't it's their problem, not yours.

Close-up on Your Ceremony Location

Before you can have a whirlwind of a time celebrating at your reception, you've got to take a deep breath, muster up all the composure you have, get ready to glide your way down that long aisle, and make it official. The ceremony itself is the heart of any wedding day. It's what makes a wedding a wedding, not just a lavish party. The ceremony sets the scene for the rest of your day, so don't leave anything to chance. The wedding of your dreams is in the details!

Once engaged, many couples get so wrapped up in where they want to have their *reception*, they initially forget to think about coordinating those dates with a ceremony location. If you're one of those people who plans to get married at the same place you have your reception, don't sweat this part. But if you're holding fast to your lifelong dream of walking down the aisle, line the church up first. Also keep in mind that different religious denominations have their own ways of preparing for the marriage process.

Going to the Chapel?

If you're having a religious ceremony, choose the location and contact your officiant about premarriage requirements as early as possible. Rules and restrictions vary not only among denominations, but also within different branches of the same religion. Individual houses of worship also have particular preferences, so work out those details.

Don't be afraid to ask your officiant questions the first time you meet. You need to understand your church's requirements. Things will go more smoothly if you and your church are on the same wavelength regarding these important issues:

- Is the date you're interested in available?
- How early or late does the church/synagogue perform ceremonies?
- What are the requirements for getting married in this church or synagogue? (Including any premarital counseling.)

- Who will perform the ceremony? (You may be close to a particular officiant, only to find that he or she is not available.)
- Are visiting clergy allowed to take part in the ceremony? If so, who will be responsible for which elements?
- Are interfaith ceremonies permitted? What are the requirements or restrictions involved?
- Are there any restrictions on decorations or music?
- Will the church or synagogue provide ceremony musicians?
- Is another wedding scheduled for the same day? If so, is there adequate time between the ceremonies?
- Are there any restrictions on where the photographer and videographer can stand (or move) during the ceremony?
- Will you be allowed to hold the receiving line at the site?

You should also ask about the cost for the ceremony and for the use of church or synagogue personnel and facilities. This donation isn't meant for any single individual; it goes to the church or synagogue as a whole.

Your officiant will be able to explain in more detail what's involved, but here's a quick rundown of the basic requirements for getting married in the various religious denominations. Once you understand what's required, then you'll be free to personalize your ceremony by choosing music, Scripture readings, special prayers, or even including your own vows.

Roman Catholic Ceremonies

A Roman Catholic ceremony consists of Introductory Rites, including opening music selections, a greeting by the priest, and an opening prayer; Liturgy of the Word, including readings by your friends and family members, and a homily that focuses on some aspect of marriage; and the Rite of Marriage, including the declaration of consent and the exchange of vows and rings. You can choose to have a complete mass that includes the Liturgy of the Eucharist, but this isn't required. You can

Classic Concerns: **Beware of No Flash**

Because flash photography can be disconcerting during a wedding ceremony, some churches and synagogues forbid it. Ask your officiant in advance—you don't want to catch flack on your wedding day.

choose other elements, such as a unity candle, particular prayers or blessings, and so on.

If you've grown up Catholic, you probably already know about the extensive premarital requirements. For starters, you need to meet with your priest and take a test. Don't worry—this isn't a pass or fail test. It's more like a personality profile that you and your fiancé each take separately. This test allows priests to compare a couple's outlook on their relationship and marriage in general. Then, at a subsequent meeting, your priest will review the results and discuss them with you. There's no need to dread this process—it can actually be quite enlightening and enjoyable, because it often sparks more in-depth conversations about many issues you and your fiancé have (hopefully) already discussed.

Then there's Pre-Cana, the premarital course that every engaged couple must complete. This course covers the big topics of marriage—sex, finances, family relationships, children—in the context of Catholicism. Despite what you might be thinking, your priest won't try to teach you about marriage. Other married couples (typically middle-aged, so they have many years of marital experience under their belts) run the courses, which usually involve group discussions with other engaged couples. When you complete the course, you'll get a certificate that says you're ready to head down the aisle.

A WORD ABOUT ANNULMENTS

If you're a divorced Catholic and you're hoping to marry again in the church, you've got your work cut out for you. You'll have to get an annulment.

This can be a long process that sometimes involves a Church investigation and possibly a trial to prove that your first marriage wasn't valid in the eyes of the Church.

The Church doesn't hand these out like popsicles. If the Church decides that your first marriage was valid, then you're out of luck. One more thing—regardless of what you've been told, if you married (and later divorced) a non-Catholic, you're not granted an automatic annulment.

Eastern Orthodox Ceremonies

The Eastern Orthodox (including Greek and Russian Orthodox) wedding ceremony is similar to the Roman Catholic one, but it features some additional rituals. Unlike Roman Catholic ceremonies, however, Eastern Orthodox marriages don't include a full mass. Services usually take place in the afternoon or evening. Many rituals in the Eastern Orthodox ceremony are performed three times, to represent the Holy Trinity.

Protestant Ceremonies

Although there are many Protestant denominations, the basic ceremony elements are the same. The officiant welcomes the guests and there is a Prayer of Blessing, followed by Scripture readings. The parents then recite a Giving in Marriage affirmation, and the bride and groom exchange vows and rings. Next, the Lord's Supper is celebrated, followed by the lighting of the unity candle, the Benediction, and the Recessional.

Protestant ceremonies generally have far fewer requirements and restrictions than Catholic marriages. An informational meeting with the clergy is required, and you might also need to take compatibility quizzes. Although premarital counseling is common, it's optional. Sunday weddings are generally discouraged. There is no need for an annulment if either party has been divorced.

Jewish Ceremonies and Preparations

Judaism, too, has different "divisions" that adhere to distinct rules. However, in the Orthodox, Conservative, and Reform traditions, certain elements are basically the same:

- The *kiddushin* (betrothal ceremony) is conducted under a *chuppah*, an ornamented canopy (optional in the Reform ceremony).
- The Seven Blessings are recited. Relatives may be chosen to read some of them.
- The bride and groom drink blessed wine; the groom then smashes the glass (wrapped in a napkin) with his foot to symbolize the fragility of life.
- Following the ceremony, the bride and groom retreat to a private room for about fifteen minutes (*yihud*)—the perfect break in a hectic day.

If you are getting married within the Orthodox or Conservative branches of Judaism, there are some stipulations. Weddings cannot take place on the Sabbath or any time that is considered holy. Both Orthodox and Conservative ceremonies are performed in Hebrew or Aramaic only; Reform ceremonies are performed in both English and Hebrew. Neither Orthodox nor Conservative branches will conduct interfaith ceremonies, although some Reform rabbis will. Men must wear yarmulkes, and the bride wears her wedding ring on her right hand. If either party is divorced, the couple is required to obtain a Jewish divorce, or *get*. Preparations for the ceremony will differ, depending on the tradition. Check with your rabbi for specific details.

Interfaith Marriages

Different religions take different stances on this matter. As mentioned above, interfaith marriage ceremonies are harder to come by in Judaism. However, the Catholic Church will sanction a marriage between a Catholic and a non-Catholic providing all of the Church's concerns are met. It is not necessary for, say, a Jewish person to convert to Catholicism in order to marry in a Catholic ceremony.

In marriages between a Protestant and a Catholic, officiants from both religions may take part in the ceremony if the couple wishes and if the church permits it. However, in a Jewish-Christian wedding, even the most liberal clergy rarely will perform a joint ceremony in the temple or church.

Let's Be Civil!

Planning an elaborate church wedding is time consuming, and when the bride and groom come from different religious backgrounds, there's potential for tension and family dissent. Not to mention that civil ceremonies are usually quite a bit easier to pull together. For those couples

Classic Concerns: **Scouting out a Civil Officiant**

A judge or some other civic official typically performs nonreligious ceremonies. If you're looking to connect quickly with an appropriate civic official who is legally qualified to perform marriages, call City Hall or your county clerk's office for information. They should be able to point you in the right direction.

The Officiant's Fee

Determining your officiant's fee is sometimes tricky. If a church official is marrying you, ask about the standard fee you'll be expected to pay. Don't assume that officiating at your wedding is part of their salary. Weddings are not considered to be part of regular duties, and the officiant should be compensated. Ceremony fees can range from $200 or $300, to closer to $1,000 in some places. Ask what the fee covers—for example, some churches include the fee for a vocalist and organist; others do not.

If your officiant doesn't want to name a figure, don't assume that something as small as twenty dollars will cut it. After all, your officiant is providing an important service.

Civil officials who perform a wedding may not be allowed to charge for their services. In this case, check before the wedding to determine if there is a fee and how much it is.

who aren't particularly religious, want to avoid the problems of an interfaith ceremony, or prefer to skip the expense and effort of a traditional church wedding, a civil ceremony might make sense.

A civil ceremony doesn't necessarily have to be boring, quick, or small. You can have all the trimmings of a traditional wedding. Move the ceremony scene out of the office—and into a hotel ballroom or a country club, onto a yacht, or anywhere else you want.

Civil ceremonies not held at City Hall or in a courthouse are often convenient, because the bride, groom, wedding party, and guests don't have to travel to a separate reception spot.

Remember that even if you do choose a civil ceremony, you still need to fulfill certain requirements. Contact your local city hall for information, but generally, you must first obtain a marriage license, and you'll need two witnesses. Also, if the officiant must travel to perform your ceremony, you should invite him or her to the reception.

Poised Under Pressure: **Secure the Location First**

Wherever you decide to get married, in most cases, you'll need to get permission in advance—and you might possibly have to pay a fee. Be sure to secure permission for the appropriate date and time before planning your entire wedding around a specific location.

Distinctive Ceremony Sites

There's no rule that says you have to get married in a traditional place of worship—even if you plan to have a religious wedding. And while some clergy might frown upon a "location" ceremony, other clergy will be more than willing to perform your ceremony where you want it. Of course, if you are not having a religious ceremony, your ceremony location is much more flexible. You'll have no trouble finding a willing officiant to perform your ceremony in a park or on a hillside.

Wide-Open Spaces

Whether you want to get married in a park, on the beach, or at the foot of a mountain, outdoor weddings can be beautiful. Just remember that you might have to work out some technical logistics in order to get your dream. In order to use most public, outdoor areas you'll first need to contact the parks commissioner, private owner, or other relevant authority to obtain permission or a permit.

Practical Magic

It's easy to get caught up in the idea of a potential wedding site because of its beauty or the unusual statement it makes. Nevertheless, consider some practicalities before committing to a site. Although the thought of taking your vows in a hot air balloon that hovers over the Grand Canyon might sound thrilling to you, it leaves little room for your loved ones, and they probably won't relish the idea of using binoculars to watch you get married. Before you choose your ceremony site, think about these things.

Space: You need to have enough room for the aisle and appropriate seating. You also need ample area for you, your groom, the officiant and anyone else to stand during the ceremony. If your heart is absolutely set on a ceremony site that will only accommodate a small number of guests, keep your ceremony small, then invite more guests to the reception.

Privacy: You might love the idea of marrying amid the historical grandeur of Grand Central Station, but you'll never have any quiet or privacy in a place like that. Even less extreme examples—such as a public park, a botanical garden, or a restaurant—might not offer the privacy you desire. Keep in mind that you will not be able to control onlookers and curiosity seekers if you choose a public forum for your ceremony.

Light and sound: If your location is dark or dim, be sure to arrange for appropriate lighting, whether it's candlelight or floodlights. Also, if any sort of loud background noise might compete with your ceremony (a waterfall, planes overhead, or foot traffic, for instance), consider using small microphones so that your guests can hear your ceremony.

Classic Rewind

Don't automatically get married in a particular place just because it's what everyone else assumes is the right thing for you to do. If you and your groom are religious, consider which church or synagogue resonates most for you. Remember, you can always ask a favorite clergy member to perform your ceremony somewhere else. Or, if that doesn't feel right to you, enlist a civil officiant to do the honors elsewhere. The most important thing is that you and your groom consider a spot that is special and personal to you both. You'll feel more comfortable about exchanging your vows and expressing your lifelong commitment to one another.

Ceremony Notes

Personal Touches

Arranging your location and meeting preceremony requirements isn't the only prep work you'll have on your mind during this time. As you approach your big day, you'll be concerned with myriad other details, such as choosing your ceremony readings and music, figuring out your wedding party processional, anticipating who sits where, and even possibly writing your own vows.

Be aware that you might encounter a few more obstacles when you get creative with your ceremony than you would with the reception. Many religions are somewhat rigid in what is permitted and not permitted in a church ceremony. But even within these parameters, there's still room to personalize your ceremony to reflect your thoughts and beliefs. Actually, unless you have a very clear idea of what you'd like to include in your ceremony, the slice of structure that your officiant provides can be a blessing.

With a little extra forethought, you and your fiancé can concoct a service that is in keeping with your beliefs, personalities, and lifestyles. Just be sure to have your officiant preapprove all of your plans.

Scripture Readings That Suit You

If you're having a religious ceremony, it will contain Scripture readings, but you don't have to recycle the same ones you've heard over and over at other weddings. Your officiant will provide you with a list of recommended readings, most of which focus on some aspect of togetherness and marriage.

If you have a favorite passage that isn't included in the list of reading selections, don't be afraid to ask about using it in your ceremony. As long as the message of the passage is appropriate for the occasion, your officiant will most likely be happy to work it into the ceremony. In fact, he or she might even be able to build a unique sermon around your favorite Biblical passage.

Music That Moves You

Music enhances the spirit and meaning of any wedding ceremony. Most officiants request that you select religious songs, but generally that doesn't mean you're confined to the music list your church gives you. If you have a favorite hymn you loved to sing in church as a child, be sure to suggest it. You might also be able to find commercially released songs that are appropriate for your ceremony "playlist."

As you consider music, keep in mind that you'll need to make selections for several phases of your ceremony.

The Prelude: This is the time when guests enter, are seated, and eagerly await your grand entrance. The prelude lasts from the time the guests start arriving until the mother of the bride is ready to make her way down the aisle. The options for music here are broad: upbeat, slow, or a mixture of both.

The Processional: This is the part where the wedding party walks down the aisle, with you entering last. A traditional march helps to set the pace for some nervous feet—but a lighter, airy piece might lift your heart as you take those first steps towards your soon-to-be-husband. You can walk to the same piece that you've chosen for the bridesmaids or to your own music. Wagner's "Bridal Chorus" is the processional that many people recall, but there are many other possibilities.

Interludes: These include any special ceremony elements, such as Communion, lighting your unity candle, exchanging rings, giving a sign of peace, or breaking the glass.

The Recessional: This is the moment you've both been waiting for—the point when you can breathe easy and stroll out arm and arm as newly married husband and wife! An up tempo song will move your guests along more quickly, so you can get your wedding show on the road.

Poised Under Pressure: **Beware of Stage Fright**

Asking a musically talented friend or relative to sing or play a special song at your wedding is a great idea. Just be sure he or she has experience performing in front of an audience and won't come down with a nasty case of stage fright on the big day.

Making a Musical Statement

There are plenty of ways to get creative with the music you include in your ceremony. The first is reinterpreting traditional classics. For instance, instead of the standard organist or string quartet, hire a different type of instrumentalist. Consider percussionists, a jazz combo, a folk singer, a xylophone player, a harmonica player, or a bagpiper. Adapt the music to suit your lifestyle, background, culture, or attitude.

Before you hire a full orchestra to accompany the church choir, remember that the cost of musicians and singers for the ceremony must fit into your overall music budget.

Sitting Pretty—at the Ceremony

Although it's not mandatory, the bride's family usually sits on the left side of the church for a Christian ceremony, while the groom's family sits on the right. The reverse is true for Reform and Conservative Jewish weddings. However, men and women are usually segregated in Orthodox Jewish ceremonies.

Ushers typically escort special guests to their seats in this order—unless otherwise directed by the bridal couple:

1. General special guests
2. Grandmothers of the bride and groom
3. Groom's mother
4. Bride's mother (unless she is also escorting the bride down the aisle with the bride's father).

Classic Concerns: **Ceremony Seating Dilemmas**

Traditionally, groomsmen have followed these specific parameters when seat-ing guests at the ceremony. However, you can certainly bend these guidelines. There's no reason why, if one side of the family is much larger than the other, the crowd can't be dispersed evenly.

Obviously, parents get first preference in the front row—or second, if the attendants will be seated during the ceremony. Any siblings not in the wedding party sit in the second row, behind your mother and father, fol-lowed by grandparents in the next row, and then other close friends and rel-atives in the fourth. The mothers of the bride and groom should be seated just before the ceremony begins.

The rest of the guests are seated as they arrive, from front to back. Ushers do not escort late-arriving guests to their seats. They should take seats near the back of the church, preferably via a side aisle.

Seating Divorced Parents

What happens in the case of divorced parents? The bride's natural mother usually has the privilege of sitting in the first row, and of selecting those who sit with her, including her spouse if she has remarried. If your divorced parents are on amicable terms, your father might sit in the second row with his spouse or significant other. If the situation is tense, however, it would be better if your father were seated a few rows back. If either one of you has been raised by your stepmother and prefer to give her the honor, she and your father might sit in the first row.

The Bride's Grand Entrance

In the past, it's always been a given that a woman's father walks her down the aisle and the mother of the bride is the last person seated before the processional begins. Nowadays, some brides are deciding to have both parents escort them down the aisle. This way, mom and dad each have their moment in the sun and bestow their blessing. In this case, both parents take their seat of honor behind the bridesmaids once the bride meets the groom and the ceremony is ready to begin.

And, while we're on the subject: Why should the groom's parents be deprived of this opportunity? Some grooms—if they're not too queasy at the thought of walking up that long aisle—also choose to be escorted in by both parents. At Jewish weddings, in fact, it's traditional for both sets of parents to escort both the bride and groom.

Special Considerations

If your father has passed on, there is really no single, easy answer to who should give you away; it's simply best to do whatever feels most comfortable to you. If your mother has remarried and you are close to your stepfather, he might be a good choice. Otherwise, a brother, a grandfather, a special uncle, or a close family friend could also do the honors. Some brides walk down the aisle with their mother or with their groom. Others choose to walk without an escort. Whomever you choose will sit in the front pew with your mother during the ceremony.

The Meaning Behind Giving the Bride Away

Back when a daughter was considered her father's possession, some formal transfer was necessary during the wedding ritual. Today, however, you'd be hard pressed to find a woman who'd concede to this sort of treatment. Now, the custom more aptly symbolizes the parents' acceptance of their daughter's passage from child to adult. Giving a daughter away signifies that the parents are bestowing their blessings on her marriage and her chosen groom.

If you are uncomfortable with the tradition where the officiant asks, "Who gives this woman . . . ?" request that your officiant asks: "Who blesses this union?"

If your parents are divorced, and you have a father and a stepfather to consider, ultimately the choice depends on your preference and your family's specific situation. To avoid risking a civil war, however, take care to include both men in the proceedings.

Receiving Your Guests

Typically, when brides and grooms are pressed for time—or patience—the receiving line is the first tradition to get cut. Truth is, it doesn't have to take up an agonizing chunk of time, and it can be quite useful. Despite your best intentions, you'll never be able to socialize at length with every guest at your wedding, especially if yours is a large one. Think of the receiving line as your insurance policy. This way, you'll be sure to have at least a bit of face time with everyone, and no one will feel left out. That fifteen or twenty minutes you put forth will buy you more dancing and eating time at the reception.

Proper Receiving Line Etiquette

Present-day receiving line etiquette is as follows: You should have one, but keep it simple. The receiving line should form some time after the ceremony but before the reception. If at all possible, try to figure in a bit of time directly following your ceremony, before your photographer whisks you off for pictures.

Poised Under Pressure: **Cut It Short**

If you're really concerned about the time it takes to have a receiving line, remember it's not imperative that every member of the wedding party stands in line. You and your groom might simply greet your guests with just your parents.

Classic Concerns: The Order of Things

Don't waste time fumbling around to form the receiving line. Follow this order: mother of the bride, father of the bride, bride, groom, mother of the groom, father of the groom. If either set of parents is divorced and there are lingering bad feelings, simply do a little reshuffling.

Just make sure to check with your officiant first; some have restrictions as to where the line may be formed. The most convenient spot is often near an exit or outside, where guests can move through easily on their way out. If you do choose to have the line at the reception site, have refreshments and entertainment available for guests while they're waiting.

If you're concerned about the receiving line dragging on, be friendly but also don't be afraid to be brief.

Writing Your Own Vows

According to Merriam-Webster, a vow is "a solemn promise or assertion . . . by which a person is bound to an act, service, or condition." And, since you are binding yourself for life in the case of marriage vows, you should be able to have *some* say in the matter. After all, you only get to stand at the altar once.

Some religions are quite strict about what they will and won't permit during the exchange of vows, so before you invest too much time writing yours, know the rules. Your officiant might help you to examine your feelings for one another, which will provide you with additional inspiration.

Today, when it comes to exchanging vows, almost anything goes. Mixing and matching traditional vows, incorporating lines of poetry, or writing them yourself are all acceptable options. The solemn nature of the vows, however, has not changed. You're still making a pledge before all of your nearest and dearest. Your goal is to express exactly what your betrothed means to you and what you are promising each other.

Finding the Right Spark

If you're up for the challenge of writing your own vows, good for you! It takes a brave person to compose personalized vows and bare his or her soul in front of so many people. Writing your own vows just requires some self-reflection and honesty. Start by thinking about your relationship and the things that have the most meaning for each of you. For example:

- How do you, as a couple, define the following terms: love, trust, marriage, family, commitment, togetherness?
- How did the two of you meet? What were the first things you noticed about each other?
- What was the single most important event in your relationship?
- Do you and your partner have a common vision of what your life together will be like as you grow older? Will it include children and grandchildren? Put that vision into words.
- Were there any obstacles to your relationship that you overcame together?
- What will life be like when you face challenges together?
- Are there any other common bonds or interests that have brought you together?
- What do you respect, love, and admire in each other?
- What about each other makes you laugh?
- How does he/she make your life complete?

Think of these ideas as seeds. It's up to you to make them grow into something more.

Put It Down on Paper

You can certainly write your vows freestyle. But if you're worried about being overwhelmed by the vow-writing process, you might want to stick to a structured formula to keep things simple. It's often better for you and your guests if you keep things short and sweet, and don't get too long-winded.

If you're feeling shy about reciting your vows at your ceremony, write them in a way that requires just a simple "I do" as a response. This way, you can still put your personal imprint on your vows without the added pressure of reciting all the words.

Revisions, Revisions

Don't worry if it takes a few drafts before you settle on the right words for your vows. At first, just give yourself permission to write anything and everything that comes to mind—you can always cut back later. After you've finished, read over your draft. Your first instincts will probably hold at least a few worthy nuggets, as these sincere, spontaneous words came straight from your heart. Now you just need to revise and give your sentiments a little structure. Think back to every tacky reality romance show you've ever watched, and take comfort in the knowledge that *anything* you write can't possibly be as bad as that.

Classic Concerns: Accentuate the Positive

When you're writing your vows, it's of utmost importance that you and your husband-to-be stay positive. Okay, maybe this seems really obvious. But we'll mention it anyway, because negativity can sometimes creep in subtly. Avoid all negative imagery; the words never *and* not *have no place in a wedding vow. Mentioning past ups and downs is usually unnecessary, and alluding to future turmoil is a surefire way to rain on your own parade.*

Outside Inspiration

What if you can't find the right words? It's not time to panic. Chances are someone else has already said exactly what you're trying to express. You might just need to find the perfect quote, poem, or song lyric to complete the mood.

The following writers have a lot to offer a bride and groom in search of great wedding-vow material.

Maya Angelou
Anne Bradstreet
Elizabeth Barrett Browning
Willa Cather
e.e. cummings
Emily Dickinson
John Donne
Ralph Waldo Emerson
Kahlil Gibran

Ben Johnson
John Keats
Anne Morrow Lindbergh
Henry Wadsworth Longfellow
John Milton
William Shakespeare
Percy Bysshe Shelley
Virgil
William Carlos Williams

Tips for Writing Great Vows

Planning a wedding can be a hard and thankless task, but writing your vows shouldn't have to be. This is one time where you can forget your stress and just focus on each other. Follow these helpful points when writing your vows, and before long, you'll have the perfect sentiments to share with your husband-to-be once you get to the altar.

Remember that your vows are a public declaration for all to hear. Be sincere and personal, but save the things that should be kept between just the two of you until later, when you're alone.

Be natural. There's no need to write your vows according to what you *think* they should sound like—make them sound like you. Although you should remain somewhat formal (no impromptu "umms," "likes," or "you know what I means"), be conversational, and speak in the style and tone you normally use.

Don't rely on memory alone to recite your vows. Write them beforehand on index cards, and ask your best man or maid of honor to hold them until the appropriate moment. Or, as mentioned above, structure your vows so that your officiant says them first, and then you simply repeat them or say, "I do."

Speak slowly and clearly. If you are marrying in an acoustically challenged venue, consider wearing mini microphones, or using the officiant's microphone when it's your turn to speak.

Classic Rewind

We've all been there countless times—the traditional church, temple, or secular wedding ceremony, listening to the same readings, songs, and vows. These places and pieces are classic, traditional, and ritualistic for a reason— the importance of the event dictates a certain gravity that these prechosen readings, vows, and songs all demonstrate. The classics also provide a sense of symbolism, tradition, and continuity from generation to generation.

However, replicating these rituals down to the last detail might not be right for every couple. Whether you want to preserve some traditional elements and then add your own flourishes, or you want to create an entirely new ceremony concept from scratch, it's up to you. Just remember that no matter if you're having a religious officiant, a judge, a ship's captain, or a justice of the peace perform your marriage, you still need to gauge his or her comfort level for the ceremony.

Extra Notes

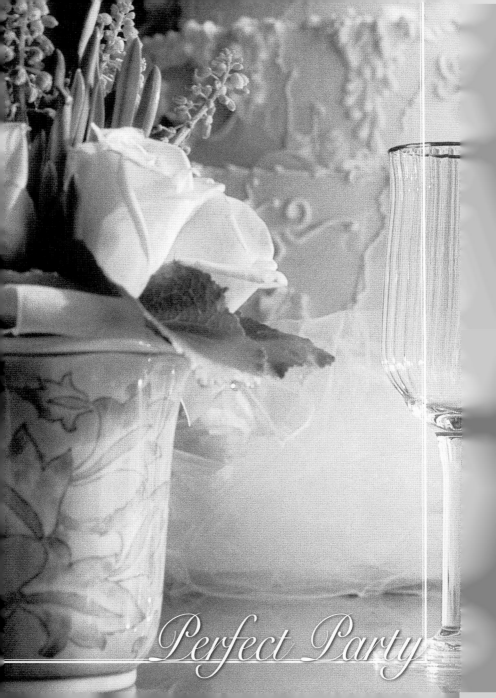

Perfect Party

party particulars

The reception is your chance to *really* have fun. It's also what's *really* going to break the bank. Make decisions about your reception carefully, but don't waste your precious time or energy agonizing.

*R*emember, wedding planning is about prioritizing, and it's tough to find one location that has every last detail you're longing for. Whatever your priorities, boil it down to what's most important to you, then follow your instincts. Before you can search for that perfect reception site, first determine what time you'd like to have your wedding. Most reception facilities offer different options depending on whether you choose to get married in the morning, at midday/mid-afternoon, or early to later evening.

Once you've zeroed in on your time of day, mix and match your options: Are you thinking breakfast/brunch sit down meal or buffet, or a buffet luncheon with hors d'oeuvres, followed by cake and coffee? Do you want a simple cocktail reception later in the afternoon, or do you prefer a full-scale five-course dinner at night? Nail down these preferences, and you'll be better equipped to find the right service provider.

One more thing to keep in mind when it comes to planning your reception: The difference between a wedding that's really great and one that's simply so-so isn't a matter of cost or extravagance. An appealing atmosphere, appetizing menu, good bar service, and fun entertainment (we'll get to that in a later section) are what make the day. Taking the time to create a reception that reflects your personalities will keep things lively and interesting. From appetizers to wedding cake and napkins to tables, this section will hit all the major points you need to think about.

Unique Options

While function halls, country clubs, and hotel ballrooms are still the most popular sites for receptions, these days there's no limit (except your imagination—and your budget, perhaps) to where you can hold your reception. As long as there's room for people to gather comfortably in a place to eat, drink, and be merry, it's fair game for the reception.

Poised Under Pressure: **A Word about the Weather**

More creative reception sites sometimes depend on the season and the weather. If Mother Nature cooperates, outdoor reception sites make the perfect backdrop for a memorable wedding day. Just be ready with a backup site elsewhere, in case you have to contend with inclement weather.

Get Creative

Looking for someplace really different for your wedding reception? Consider these unusual settings:

- Castles, estates, or historic mansions
- Observatories
- Museums/art galleries
- Scenic mountain resorts
- Historic battleships, boats, or yachts
- Garden, greenhouses, or public parks
- Concert halls or theaters

Let your common interests guide you, then follow up with some phone calls to the appropriate people (the manager of the historic movie theater, for example) to find out what's available in your area. Odds are you'll pay more to secure one of these nontraditional sites. Weigh the cost against what you'll be getting for your money.

Theme Come True

Maybe you're brave enough to pull off a Renaissance-themed wedding—and bold enough to convince your groom to don tights. If so, go with that flow (just remember to fill your guests in on the details). But a reception that resembles a scene from a Shakespearean sonnet is not the only way to play on an interesting theme. Also consider these options:

- **An ethnic wedding:** You and your fiancé could highlight the culture and costumes of your ethnic backgrounds.

- **A holiday wedding:** Weddings during the holidays allow you to take advantage of great decorations and high spirits.

- **An all-night wedding:** If you and your groom want to make things last, plan to celebrate straight through the night. These weddings usually come to a close with breakfast the next morning.

- **A weekend wedding:** These celebrations last all weekend long. Weekend weddings are often set up like a mini-vacation for you and your guests, and they take place at a resort or hotel.

Whether it's hockey or Hawaii that thrills you, pick your theme, and then carry it through all aspects of your wedding.

Classic Style

Don't worry—you don't have to dress up in costumes or have a hobby-themed wedding to make yours memorable. No matter where or how you decide to receive your guests as husband and wife, that spot will seem like the most perfect place on Earth on your wedding day.

Poised Under Pressure: **No Sweat!**

Let's be clear here: Home reception does not equal backyard barbeque. The last thing you want to do is make your parents and other family members sweat in the kitchen all week long before your wedding, preparing food for the reception. If you're having more than fifty guests, hire a professional caterer.

There's No Place Like Home

If you, your parents, or someone you know has a house and yard big enough to accommodate your reception, you could be in luck. A place that's filled with childhood memories is wonderful when filled with family and friends for your wedding day.

If you and your groom aren't much for fluff and fuss, a backyard reception might be a safe bet, because these receptions are much less formal. They can also be much less expensive—you won't be tied down with including typical wedding trimmings or adhering to a formal dress code.

Stay Put!

When convenience is your primary consideration, a reception held on the same grounds as the ceremony might be in order. Many churches and synagogues have a function room that you can rent for a lot less than a commercial site. These receptions are typically small and informal, so don't expect to invite 200 guests. Keep in mind that when it comes to refreshments, we're talking cookies and punch, or a small buffet lunch. If a five-course meal is what you're after, start looking elsewhere. Bear in mind that a site with a religious affiliation might not allow alcohol and might put restrictions on the kinds of music you can play at the reception.

You can have a big, fancy wedding, and still stay in one place. For a large wedding where many guests are traveling in from out of town, it makes perfect sense to have your reception at a hotel. This way, you can get a banquet facility and room accommodations in one fell swoop, and no one has to do any more traveling once the reception's over.

The Waiting Game

You've found the perfect place for your ceremony and the perfect place for your reception. The only problem is, the reception site is booked until two hours after your ceremony ends.

Relax. No law says the reception *must* start immediately following the ceremony. Just make sure that your guests have something to do if the downtime is considerable. If your guests are mostly local, they might go home for a break between the ceremony and reception. But if you have many out-of-town guests, be ready to provide suggestions. Set up a hospitality suite at the hotel where guests are staying, or ask a close friend or relative to have cocktails or hors d'oeuvres at his or her house. Close family members and friends might want to tag along if you plan to take pictures at a certain location. Weather permitting, in that case you might consider asking someone to bring a cooler with bottles of water or soda and some light snacks as refreshments. Also be ready to suggest nearby restaurants or coffee shops, if people are looking for somewhere to hang out before the reception begins.

Finding the Right Reception Site

For you and your groom, your wedding is a personal, romantic event. To those vendors and service providers with whom you work, however, it's all one big business transaction. Be prepared to ask any potential banquet facility manager as many specific questions as possible.

- ◆ How many people can the facility comfortably seat? How big is the dance floor?

- ◆ Is an in-house catering service offered? If so, what in particular is included in the various sit-down and buffet options? Can you bring in your own caterer? (See section on catering for more details.)

- ◆ If the reception facility provides the catering, what is the cost per plate, and does that price include tax and gratuity? What about dinners for vendors, or children's plates? Are vegetarian options available, if requested?

- ◆ For what length of time will the facility be available? Is there a time minimum you must meet? Are there overtime charges?

Classic Concerns: Movin' to the Country

Avoid receptions right in a city if you can—it's less expensive if you have your reception on the outskirts. And don't turn your nose up at the potential for a great wedding in your own home area. There are lots of great places, if you look for them.

- Is there free parking? If there is valet parking, what are the rates and gratuities?

- Will there be coatroom and restroom attendants? A bartender? A doorman? What are the charges?

- Are there any additional charges for the staff's working time?

- If you've arranged for an open bar, do you have to provide the alcohol? If you've arranged for a cash bar, what will the prices be?

- Does the facility have more than one reception site on the premises? Is yours the only reception happening that day or are other receptions booked before or at the same time as yours?

- How much of a deposit is required? Will your deposit be returned in the event of a cancellation?

Ask any and all questions as they come to you. Consider where your musicians will set up, how many tables will be necessary to accommodate the number of guests you plan to have, whether or not table linens, chair covers, table centerpieces, or other decorations are included, and so on.

Shop Around

Save time by asking some of the preliminary questions listed above over the phone. There's no use actually visiting a reception site if it can't accommodate your number of guests or its price is out of your range. When you do visit locations, be sure to bring this organizer with you, so that you can write down all of the answers to your questions and compare notes later.

Keeping Tabs: First Impressions

As you meet with the managers of various banquet facilities you're considering, don't underestimate the power of first impressions. Were the people who met with you courteous and responsive, or curt and disinterested? Your wedding-planning experience will be infinitely better if you feel comfortable with the staff at your facility and confident in their abilities.

If you like a particular facility and the prices quoted, go back to see a wedding or another formal dinner in progress. Sample food selections, or at least dig for feedback on the food from family members or friends who've been there before. Have dinner there on a Saturday or Sunday, when presumably the kitchen and staff are putting forth their best efforts at their busiest time.

Once you're really interested in a certain place, ask the site manager to work up a preliminary estimate, and get it in writing. Make sure he or she spells out the details of the menu, service, and anything else you've discussed. Compare various estimates and impressions before you commit. Also, don't be afraid to ask a facility to hold your chosen date. Most will be glad to give you a week or two to mull things over.

Paying the Piper

We've said it before, but it bears repeating: Make sure you're aware of all reception-related charges up front. When you forget to add in tax, gratuity, or extra charges, it can break your budget. Cancellations, changes, and last-minute additions also tack on unwanted costs. Be as organized and prepared for things as possible *before* booking your site.

Once all of the details are settled, that leaves just one more matter to contend with: that not-so-tiny detail called the deposit. A deposit—usually a great big one—will reserve the site you want. Many sites won't refund this deposit if you decide you don't want to go with them after all. Before you sign on the dotted line, review the agreement carefully, and check references.

Reception Notes

Table Talk

Unless you're planning a cocktail reception with hors d'oeuvres or an informal buffet, you're going to need a seating chart. Guests (especially those who don't know many people) often feel uncomfortable without assigned seating, and, if you're having a large reception, you're just asking for mass chaos without one.

Get input from both families; if possible, you should all come up with the plan together. Both moms will know which relatives will want to sit together—and which should be seated at opposite ends of the room. This will make *your* life easier.

Placing People

If you're planning a very formal wedding, place cards are necessary for all guests. At less formal receptions, place cards are used only at the head table. The easiest way to alert guests to their table assignments is to place table cards on a table near the reception room entrance. Table cards simply list the name of the guest and their table assignment.

Some reception facilities provide place cards for you, while others expect you to provide them yourself. Be sure to check with your reception facility about how to write up your seating chart, where the tables will be placed, how many guests are seated at each table, and so on. Your reception manager will explain exactly how you should set things up.

Classic Concerns: **Easy Table ID**

Here's an idea for creative seating assignments: Decorate the tables with centerpieces and other goodies that go along with different themes, then name the tables accordingly. For instance, if you put a different type of floral arrangement at each table, you can tell your guests that they'll be sitting at the Daisy table or the Rose table.

Save Me a Seat!

Traditionally, the bride and groom, honor attendants, bridesmaids, and ushers sit at the head table. The bride and groom sit in the middle, with the best man next to the bride and the maid of honor next to the groom. The head table usually faces the other tables and is sometimes elevated.

There are other options, however. You might choose to have a table for two—just you and your groom. Or you could sit with your honor attendants at one table and cluster the rest of your attendants around you at a few other smaller tables. This option works well for larger wedding parties, and might also give you the option of seating your bridesmaids and groomsmen with their significant others who aren't in the wedding party.

The Parents

There's no single correct seating arrangement for the parents' tables—it's up to you to use your own judgment here. The bride and groom's parents can sit together with the officiant and his or her spouse at the parents' table, or each set of parents can host their own table with close family members, such as the grandparents, godparents, or other close friends.

What should you do if your parents are divorced, and they're actively warring? The trick here is to put each of them with their own family and friends at separate tables that are both in the vicinity of the head table, yet not so close to *each other* that they'll have reason to cross paths. Your parents and stepparents are adults and they should be expected to behave as such. If they try to make a drama out of your wedding (threatening not to attend if the other ex-spouse attends, for instance), don't give in to the ploy.

Reception Highlights

Hopefully by this point you know how to work out all of your preliminary arrangements, so it's on to the actual event. There are several familiar rituals that take place at a wedding reception. Take them, leave them, it's up to you to decide what works best at your reception . . .

Don't forget that your reception is what you make of it. Aside from the standard traditions like dancing with parents, giving toasts, and cutting the cake, you can also add any other traditions or activities you like.

The Toasts

Toasts, of course, are an important part of the wedding reception—and, like every other wedding ritual, toasting has its etiquette. Traditionally, the best man is first in line. But that doesn't mean others can't chime in as well. Nowadays, the maid or matron of honor often gives a toast. And, if either of the bride or groom's parents have something to say, great! Just be sure to instruct everyone to be appropriate in their presentation (watch for embarrassing stories from the best man here), and to keep it short, if several people want to say a *few* words.

In case all of your family and friends are anxiously awaiting their chance to hail you and your groom at the reception, the order of toasters is as follows: best man, groom's dad, bride's dad, groom, bride, maid or matron of honor, groom's mom, bride's mom . . . and then any other family members or friends. (Good luck to you, at this point!)

Once the toasts are given, dinner is served!

The Opening Dances

Once the band or DJ announces the wedding party, the bride and groom usually share their first dance. This is a sentimental moment, as you and your new husband dance to the song the two of you have carefully chosen while your guests look on and smile.

Later on, the bride dances with her father, and then the groom dances with his mother. Then it's on to dances with the new in-laws, dances with the wedding party . . .

That's a whole lot of dancing, you say? It sure is—and it can be time consuming, especially when you know your guests are just itching to hit the dance floor. Just be sure to take the time to dance with all of the people who are important to you—as you dance, you'll be able to steal a few private moments with not just your dad, but your brothers, grandfathers, and uncles, too. In years to come, you'll remember those dances as some of the best parts of your wedding day.

Feel free to eliminate or combine some or all of these dances, or intersperse them throughout the evening, perhaps in between meal courses. When you're ready to mambo with the masses, make sure the master of ceremonies announces that *everyone* is welcome on the dance floor.

Poised Under Pressure: A Little Practice

You probably want to choose a first-dance song that resonates with meaning for you both. But that's not the only thought to bear in mind—also consider the length and tempo of the song. Above all, practice dancing to your song before your big moment. You want to be prepared for how long you two will have to sway to the music, as well as what type of fancy footwork (or lack thereof) you'll use to maneuver through it!

The Cake Cutting

This is the moment everyone has been waiting for. The question: To smash, or not to smash (in each other's faces, that is)? At a sit-down reception, the cake is usually cut right before the dessert (if any) is served; however, if you have a photographer who is trying to expedite things, don't be surprised if he or she wants to move the cake-cutting up a bit. Once you slice the first piece to some cute music of your choice and then feed each other, the cater-er or baker will cut the rest of the cake and distribute it.

The Bouquet and Garter Toss

Once widely accepted traditions, these reception elements have gradually lost favor in some circles. Whatever possessed someone to decide it was a good idea for the bride to toss the bouquet to the single ladies and the groom to throw the garter to the single guys, then proceed to have the two "lucky winners" come together in the middle of the dance floor, is beyond all reason. All the men might cheer as the guy with the garter slides it up, up, up the single lady's leg, but mostly, the other women are just grateful they weren't the ones to catch the bouquet.

Today, many brides find this tradition distasteful, especially for the women involved, and decide to eliminate it, in whole—or at least in *part*. Consider asking all the married couples at your wedding to join you and your groom for an anniversary dance. Have your band leader or DJ ask couples who've been married less than a certain number of years to leave the dance floor through the course of the song, until at the end, you are left with the couple who's been married the longest. Presenting this cou-ple with your toss bouquet is a fitting way to pay tribute to the institution of marriage.

Classic Rewind

Keep in mind that depending on which part of the country you live in, you might have to move fast on your decision about a reception facility, or else risk losing your chosen date. This is not to say you should make a hasty judgment. Gather as much information as possible, pay attention to what you see and how you feel when you visit each location, and then move on it. No matter where you are when you celebrate your day, remember that you're there celebrating your commitment to each other surrounded by all the people that matter most to you.

In-House Caterers

If you're lucky, your reception site will have an in-house catering staff that serves great food and knows how to work well with you. Hotels offer these services, as do most country clubs and other banquet facilities. There are several advantages to using an in-house caterer, the main one being that you don't have to find a separate service and then coordinate the details yourself. Plus, in-house catering staffs are already familiar with the particulars of their banquet rooms, which is a huge advantage.

But the in-house picture isn't *all* rosy. For starters, in-house catering is usually more expensive than independent catering. Some reception facilities might charge you for lots of little extras you may not want or need as part of one all-inclusive package price. Best-case scenario, you'll be offered a variety of food packages at different price levels, or you'll be given the option of adding and removing options à la carte.

But it's not always that simple. Some reception facilities might not allow you to adapt your package, or give you the option of employing another catering service. Most times, with these types, it's their way or the highway. If the food is good and the price is reasonable, you might find this arrangement completely acceptable. However, if during your taste test you determine that the food is terrible, move on!

Independent Caterers

If you decide to have your reception outdoors or at some other nontraditional site, the task of feeding the restless natives will probably fall to you and your groom. Before you start searching for an independent caterer, find out what your reception site provides—and what it doesn't. Some sites offer linens, glass and dinnerware, tables, chairs—everything but the food. Others provide nothing but the space you'll be celebrating in. Know what you need *before* you go looking so nothing slips through the cracks.

No-Frills Caterers

Some caterers keep it simple and provide just the food, period. Sometimes this can work to your advantage, especially if the caterer offers great food at a low price, and then you're able to hunt around to find good deals on everything else you need. The disadvantage is that all of this scavenging can be very inconvenient, especially when you're faced with all the other tasks it takes to plan a wedding. Decide what you can handle. If you're a savvy businesswoman and you don't mind making lots of calls, you might do fine this way; but if you absolutely abhor shopping around, it could be a logistical mess.

In-Between Caterers

This type of caterer provides everything for the reception, including food, beverages, a wait staff, and bartenders. Most also offer linens and dinnerware.

Poised Under Pressure: **Rental Equipment**

If your reception site doesn't provide tables, chairs, or other equipment, you'll have to scout out your options and determine fair prices for yourself, then figure out how to get it all to the reception site and return it afterward. Be prepared and allow yourself enough time to coordinate.

Keeping Tabs: **Ask about Appetizers**

If you're looking to have a lot of hors d'oeuvres at your reception but your caterer doesn't include them in a package, get a price list before you start adding all sorts of things to your menu. Also be aware if there is a price difference between setting the appetizers out on a table where guests serve themselves, and having the wait staff pass them around on trays.

If you need tables and chairs, these caterers will usually do the legwork and simply add that to the cost of your total bill. If you're lucky, they'll charge you exactly what the rental agency charged them, but it's probably more likely that they'll add a fee. Get a written estimate before you authorize *anything*. Some of these caterers will allow you to supply the alcohol yourself, because they prefer not to worry about the potential liability (or their loss of liquor revenue).

The Heavyweights

As you would expect, these hard-core caterers offer just about every item and service you can imagine, and a few you probably can't. Many have branched out into the reception coordinating business. Basically, if you choose to pay them for it, they'll take on the entire responsibility of planning your reception, including music, flowers, photographer—the whole nine yards. This might sound like a dream come true at first, but unless you're careful, it has the potential to become a nightmare.

First, this kind of service doesn't come cheap. Second, you're flying blind. When you do all of your research yourself, you feel more confident about the service providers you hire. But if your catering service sets you up with a photographer, for instance, how are you to know whether you'll get a high-quality professional, or just some amateur with a nice camera who happens to be a close friend of your chef? Then there is the question of quality. With so many irons in so many fires, even seasoned veterans can make horrendous mistakes. If you find a "fat" catering service that appeals to you, consider contracting them for the traditional catering services— but keep tight control over everything else.

Grilling Your Caterer

No matter what type of caterer you decide to go with, ask questions to make sure they can provide proper services. Once again, don't be a shy bride—the success of your wedding (and your hard-earned money) is at stake.

First of all, you need to know the price of the food you're ordering. Initially, caterers can give you an estimate based on current food prices; then, closer to the wedding, they should supply a final quote reflecting prices at that time. Also ask how much of a difference you should expect—you don't want to pay $50 for a meal your caterer originally quoted as $25.

Don't forget to find out if the estimate you're quoted includes meals for your disc jockey (or an entire band), your photographer, your videographer, and any other service providers on the clock that evening. And remember to pay attention to the refund policy!

Classic Concerns: **Kitchen Check**

If you're hiring a caterer to do the food for a wedding at home, make sure your service checks out the kitchen, appliances, storage, and electrical capabilities to ensure that there's enough space and power to work properly. Although your mother's tiny kitchen might be fine when cooking for just the family, you need to be certain it can handle ten people preparing and serving massive amounts of food.

Dinner Is Served

No matter how simple or fancy the service, you want to know what choices you have, and whether a caterer can meet your needs. Ask about the different options available. Here are some common food considerations:

◆ Will your guests have a choice of entrée?

◆ Does your facility specialize in any particular cuisine?

◆ Are hors d'oeuvres included in your food package?

◆ If you're contemplating a buffet, is it practical to serve food this way, based on the number of guests you're inviting?

◆ If you're having a sit down dinner, how many courses are included?

◆ If you have vegetarian or kosher guests attending the reception, can special meals be prepared for them?

◆ Is your wedding cake included in your catering package? Will your caterers provide the cake themselves, or will they send you to a separate bakery?

◆ Will the caterer charge you a "cake cutting" fee? If so, get out of it, or find another caterer. This supposed "service fee" is nothing but an excuse to charge more money!

- What happens with all your leftover food? Can you and your guests take it home? Could you donate it to a local charity?
- When must you supply them with your final guest count?
- Can you taste your meal options before making your selections?

Once you find a caterer who meets your budget and needs, *get every part of your agreement in writing*. Ask for references, and leave no stone unturned, so you don't get tripped up right before the wedding.

Sit Down or Buffet?

A sit-down meal is generally considered more formal than a buffet. But, if you're leaning toward a buffet, that does have its advantages: It's usually less expensive to serve, because it eliminates the need for waiters and waitresses. And a buffet meal can add a relaxed touch to a morning or afternoon wedding. Before you make up your mind, discuss your options with your caterer. This choice at least in part depends on the size of your reception site and the number of guests you're having. Buffets aren't so tedious when there are only fifty guests to feed. But a buffet for 200 or more could unravel into chaos!

Remember, buffet service does require more food than a sit-down meal, since portions are not controlled. You need to put out plenty of food so that no one will feel shy about taking enough to eat.

Poised Under Pressure: **Sit-Down Buffet Combo**

If you're having trouble deciding between a sit-down dinner and a buffet, why not combine the best of both? Some facilities will serve certain parts of the meal, such as the salad and entrée, sit-down style, but also include additional courses, such as a pasta station, in their package. This allows you to offer a full range of food while still moving the meal along quickly.

Poised Under Pressure: **Other Catering Concerns**

Beyond the specifics of the food itself, you'll want to know what the ratio of staff to guests will be, and what the staff will be wearing. Also ask about the linens, dinnerware, and other related items. If you're planning a pink wedding, the last thing you want is brown tablecloths!

Food Stations

This option is gaining popularity. Rather than one large buffet table, with this option, several manned food stations are set up around the reception hall. Common stations include:

◆ A pasta station with a variety of pasta and sauce choices, which the chef cooks up for each guest individually.

◆ A carving station offers a selection of meats carved right from the bone, including turkey, beef, or ham.

◆ A skewer station provides a great combination of vegetables and meats or seafood. Cooking each individual skewer can be slightly more time-consuming than a pasta or carving station; the alternative is to have the skewers preflamed, and then presented buffet style.

If you want to get more creative with food stations, try these:

◆ A Mexican taco or burrito station

◆ A Thai food or Chinese food station

◆ A hibachi-style Japanese station

◆ A sushi station

◆ An omelet or French crepe station

Memorable Menus

To some guests, food is the most important ingredient for an enjoyable wedding. It's surprising, then, that so many couples continue to choose the same old safe entrées prepared in familiar ways. To be fair, many brides and grooms choose to err on the side of caution, serving time-tested crowd pleasers. However, if your guests are open-minded and you'd like to branch out, make a statement with your menu.

Also talk to your caterer about introducing unusual presentation methods, such as appetizers served in chilled martini glasses, soups ladled into bread bowls or hollowed out pumpkins or gourds, sorbet served in melon shells, or any other creative serving methods they might have.

Can't choose between two great-sounding entrees? Here's a simple solution: Serve both in slightly smaller portions, such as a steak with fish, or chicken with a pasta dish.

Original Hors d'Oeuvres

The way in which hors d'oeuvres are served can be as interesting as the food itself, They can be served in an elegant butler-passed style; at a large, central spread; or at stations placed throughout the reception site. If you choose to have butler-passed hors d'oeuvres, consider serving standard favorites along with less common selections.

If you decide to have a large, centrally located spread or stations during cocktail hour, consider theming them—for instance, plan a nautical theme for seafood, or include Japanese-inspired décor with a sushi table.

The Wedding Cake

Today's wedding cakes can cost anywhere from hundreds to even thousands of dollars. The good news is that cake designers are getting much more creative, and couples are deviating from the standard white, over-the-top creation with fountains, lots of frosting, and ceramic cake topper. Here are some considerations you should be sure to cover with your baker:

- Give your bakery a count of how many guests you're having.
- Find out if a deposit is required; if so, how much?
- Ask about any delivery or set-up fees.
- If you want someone from the bakery to stay at the reception to cut and serve your cake, find out how much this will cost.
- Get a written contract detailing the type of cake, cost, date of delivery, and other important details.
- Coordinate with your reception site and baker to determine where the cake should be displayed.

As you begin consulting with cake designers, consider these creative ideas. Then be sure the one you choose has the requisite capabilities.

Color

White is no longer the limit when it comes to cakes. Options range from fairly traditional styles with a bit of trim color, to cake layers stacked in different shades and patterns, like plaids and polka dots. Most cake designers can incorporate your wedding colors or any other hue you favor.

Poised Under Pressure: **Let Yourself Eat Cake!**

Nothing soothes the savage beast within like cake testing. This is one of the most enjoyable aspects of wedding planning. Ask to taste test any style of cake you're seriously considering for your wedding. Most reputable bakers plan to have selections ready when you meet with them. You'll have fun tasting, and you'll be sure that your guests won't be filling their bellies with a lead weight.

You might also consider livening up your white cake with other decorative additions, such as bright flowers between tiers or strewn atop the cake, or ribbons and bows (actual or made of edible gum paste).

Shape

While round cakes are classic and beautiful, you don't have to have a cake in this shape. The right cake designer can make a cake of any shape and size. Whatever your interests, your cake can reflect it—a tennis racquet, a musical instrument, a sailboat, a flower blossom, a bicycle. Just remember how costly cakes can be, and decide whether it's worth shelling out an exorbitant amount.

Flavor

Why stick to plain old vanilla? Most cake designers and bakers have a wider variety than ever to choose from, such as carrot cake, mud cake, Italian rum cake, cheesecake, spice cake, coffee cake, pound cake, chocolate mousse—even ice cream cakes. Not to mention all those filling options—raspberry, strawberry, lemon, custard, buttercream . . . . If you're having a traditional tiered cake, switch things up by including a different flavor for each tier. You could honor your mom, dad, or grandparents by including the flavors you know are their favorites; some bakers will even use a favorite family cake recipe if you request it.

Classic Concerns: Say No to Extra Dessert

You don't need more than your wedding cake for dessert. An additional dessert buffet might sound tempting ahead of time, but you're not going to like it when you're left at the end of your reception with a table still nearly full with expensive cookies and pastries. Eliminating extra dessert can save you an extra $3 to $5—or more—per guest.

Variety

So cake's not your favorite desert? Not a problem—create your own wedding tradition by serving some other dessert. Or include a small cake among an extensive table of pastries, chocolates, cookies, tarts, éclairs, and other fancy desserts, so guests can take their pick.

All the Extras

Don't forget to get creative with your cake accoutrements, such as the stand or pedestal and cake knife and server. Use family heirlooms, or shop for something in an unusual color or style. And don't forget your cake table—decorate it with flowers, balloons, candles, or a collection of framed family photos.

No law says you have to have the standard bride-and-groom topper on your cake. Your cake topper is a great way to reflect your interests as a couple—if you're pet lovers, use animal figurines, or if you're sports enthusiasts, go that route.

Cocktail Time

Deciding what to do about bar service is always a hot topic. Should you have an open bar, where guests drink free, or a cash bar, where each guest has to buck up per drink? While some point out the indisputable fact that open bars can be extremely expensive, there's no getting around that it's rude to expect guests to pay for their own drinks. (You wouldn't ask them to pay for their dinners, would you?)

The least expensive way to serve alcohol at your wedding is to do it yourself. Because many reception sites don't allow this (restaurants and halls with caterers onsite, in particular), be sure to check in advance. If this is permitted, however, it might be financially advantageous if you sidestep the caterer's markups and only pay for what is consumed. Just bear in mind that the fee-per-person-per-hour pay schedule often ends up being much more expensive than what was actually imbibed. Factor in the other additional costs, such as shipping the liquor to the site, setting up the bar, renting glasses and barware, and paying a bartender's fee.

Affordable Options

Unlike your college friends who still consider Rolling Rock the way to go, bar snobs or serious drinkers will notice what you're serving. If you've got top-shelf taste but a bottom-shelf budget, there are creative ways to serve the good stuff without breaking the bank (or even worse—including a cash bar).

- **Have an open bar for the first hour of the reception only.** This will help your guests pass the time while you're off taking pictures.
- **Serve an abbreviated drink selection.** A fully stocked bar is unnecessary for a luncheon reception. In that case, mimosas, champagne or champagne punch, bloody marys, or other light drinks are more appropriate.
- **Place bottles of wine on the tables.** A typical bottle of wine holds four to five glasses. At a table for eight, a bottle of red and white ensures that everyone gets a glass or two with their meal. You control the expense and the amount of consumption by purchasing a set number of bottles of the wines of your choice.
- If your reception site allows it, purchase a few kegs or several cases of high-quality beer plus some cases of good wine.

Tray Cool

Tray service is another possible option. This way, your guests don't have to pay for their drinks, and you don't incur the massive expense of an open bar. Choose a few drinks (beer and wine are sure bets). Then, the wait staff will pass these selections around on a tray and offer them to your guests. Rather than float around all night, the servers bring drinks around on a schedule to keep costs (and excessive consumption) to a minimum.

Food and Catering Notes

Do-It-Yourself Bartending

If you're having a home or backyard reception, and you've chosen to provide alcohol yourself (instead of leaving it to the caterer), you'll need to know what you need and how much of it to have on hand. If you're serving alcohol for an at-home reception, it must be an open bar. It's against the law to sell liquor without a license, so don't mess this up.

Now, for the beverages and other items you'll actually need . . .

- **Champagne or sparkling white wine:** Though we commonly refer to any sparkling white wine as champagne, only the wine made in the Champagne region of France actually carries this title. You'll pay more for good champagne, but you can pick up a decent sparkling wine for around $10. Typically, you only need enough champagne to fill everyone's glass once for the opening toast.

- **The staples:** Of course, you'll need plenty of beer and wine on hand.

- **The hard stuff:** Essentials such as vodka, gin, rum, tequila, vermouth, and blended whiskey should be enough to please everybody. But if you're inviting a crowd who enjoys schnapps, brandy, or more unusual cocktails adjust your shopping list accordingly.

- **Nonalcoholic options:** Be sure to have things like soft drinks, punch, and sparkling grape or apple juice on hand for guests who prefer to steer clear of the hard stuff.

- **Garnishes:** You're not through yet. Once you have all the alcohol, you still need things like maraschino cherries, lemons, limes, celery, and olives. Also don't forget mixers like soft drinks, soda water, tonic water, and milk, as well as other accoutrements such as ice, swizzle sticks, and cocktail napkins.

Running the Numbers

Figure that on average, each guest will have four to five drinks in an evening. Based on that, here are some general estimates to help you anticipate how much you'll need:

- A fifth of liquor will give you twenty-five drinks, providing you're making them with one ounce of alcohol each; using one-and-a-half ounces of alcohol, you'll get eighteen drinks per fifth.

- A single case of liquor contains twelve bottles. Assuming that you're using one ounce of alcohol to make every drink, then one case will yield 300 drinks.

- One-half of a keg will give you 260 eight-ounce glasses of beer.

- If you're serving beer in bottles and cans instead of on tap, seven cases is the equivalent of one-half keg.

- A bottle of champagne yields seven glasses.

- As already noted, a typical bottle of wine serves four to five glasses. But if certain members of your crowd really love to drink wine, it's best to figure those party animals will each consume the equivalent of one full-sized bottle.

Poised Under Pressure: **Drunken Damage Control**

A bunch of rowdy drunks is the last thing you want—they're a hazard to themselves, everyone else, and your wedding! Feed these lushes meat, fish, cheese, and other high-protein foods; they restore blood sugar, which is depleted when drinking alcohol, and help to sober up guests who've had a little too much bubbly. Coffee only wires a drunk, so if you're trying to sober someone up, make him or her drink water instead—it will flush out his or her system.

Your Liability as a Host

If you're serving liquor at your reception, you need to be aware of your responsibilities. First of all, liquor may not be served to anyone under age, even at a home party. Courts have ruled that hosts are financially liable when teenagers who are served liquor at parties in private homes become involved in auto accidents or criminal matters. Caterers and restaurants have been held to the same rule.

Adult guests who are too drunk to drive but do so, and have an accident after being served drinks at your party, are also your responsibility and liability. Caterers and bartenders are liable in this situation, as well.

Discuss ways to limit alcohol consumption at your reception with your caterer. Reliable caterers are happy to cooperate and usually come prepared with methods for doing so.

Bartending Extras

Bent on serving up a top-notch bar spread? There are plenty of creative and unusual touches you can incorporate.

◆ Include a separate martini bar, where guests can order martinis in all the latest flavors—melon, lemon, lime, chocolate, and, of course, cosmos.

◆ Serve other "spotlight" drinks, such as a frozen drinks or the bartender's secret-recipe sangria.

◆ Play up seasonal favorites with premade pitchers of, say, gin and tonic and sloe gin fizz for summer; hard cider for fall; or eggnog for winter.

◆ Include choices that reflect your ethnic heritage or your honeymoon destination. For example, serve a selection of Irish beers like Guinness and Harp, Mexican beers like Dos Equis or Corona, Jamaican Red Stripe beer, Belgian beers, Russian or Polish vodka, Italian grappa or wine, or Japanese sake.

Classic Rewind

Catering options can run a full gamut, from two people in a kitchen preparing sandwiches and hors d'oeuvres for an at-home reception, to a full-service facility that coordinates your entire reception—food, full bar, tables, chairs, dinnerware, and matching linens, to boot. Amenities aside, however, the most important thing is the quality of food. A caterer can be friendly, inexpensive, cooperative, and downright artistic—but if his food doesn't taste good, you might as well forget it. Don't subject your guests to bad food for the sake of a great deal. You don't have to serve an extravagant dinner, but you do want food that's worth the money you'll pay for it.

Bartending Notes

Essential Tips

In This Section:

Essential Tips

Vendors and Other Essentials

Music

Photography

Videography

Classic Style

Flowers

Transportation

Invitations

Additional Pertinent Details

Chapter Five

vendors and other essentials

The key to a glorious and successful wedding day is in the details, details, details! So many elements come into play when planning your big day, and now is the time to get down to the business of making smart decisions.

You may have made it to Part 3 in this organizer, but you've still got a lot of coordinating to do. Sure, you've probably lined up things for your ceremony and reception, and hopefully you have a handle on your budget. But what about all of the other elements that go into making a memorable wedding day? You need to choose the dresses and tuxes, line up your entertainment, ensure your wedding photos will be great, get yourself to the church on time, and take care of legal logistics, too. Think of this section as your step-by-step guide to arranging these key details.

Music

Whether you're as graceful as Ginger Rogers or a former wallflower with two left feet, music will set the tone for your celebration. Music is highly subjective, so be clear on what you're looking for in this department, lest you end up with a musical host akin to Adam Sandler at his worst in *The Wedding Singer*. Do you prefer a DJ or a band? Are you looking for music that will unleash your guests' inner disco divas, or is swing more your thing? Ask the right questions before you sign on the dotted line, so you're sure the entertainment won't run amok.

Pick Your Playlist

Selecting the right entertainer for your reception is a tough job since you need to satisfy a wide cross section of people. Mom and Dad insist on Frank Sinatra and The Four Tops, Grandma and Grandpa want Big Band, your Aunt Sally's set for "Saturday Night Fever," and your younger cousins are begging for Britney Spears. On top of all that, you have your friends to consider—and where do your own tastes fit? Finding that happy medium is no small feat. No wonder so many couples go with a DJ or a "wedding" band who can play favorites from James Brown to James Taylor.

Who's Your Music Man?

The size, formality, and budget of your wedding should help you to determine the type of entertainment you choose. A very formal affair might have a strolling violinist or a piano player who provides background music as the meal is served, while a backyard reception might simply use homemade CDs piped through a good stereo system. Your priorities will be quite different if you're looking for a celebrity DJ who spins the latest and greatest club favorites, versus a swing band that croons smooth tunes.

When deciding between a band or DJ, keep in mind the size of the space you'll have. If your reception location is on the small side, there might

Classic Concerns: Show Stoppers

Beware of cheesy DJs and band emcees who make themselves the center of attention. Also make sure the person acting as emcee has the poise and charisma to handle the responsibility. You don't want to turn the microphone over to someone who will insult your guests, make bad jokes as you cut the cake, or mumble your names unintelligibly. Get a solid recommendation or watch them in action before you commit.

not be enough room for a ten-member band. A DJ's equipment will take up less space.

Since many bands and DJs *don't* advertise, word of mouth means a lot. If, after asking around, you're still hard pressed, talk to your reception site coordinator. He or she has probably seen a lot of musical entertainment come and go and might be able to recommend someone.

These days, the big musical decision is whether to hire a band or a DJ. A DJ will typically be less expensive than a band, because you are paying for one person's time rather than five to ten band members' time. If you want live music, keep in mind that the smaller the band, the less expensive their fee—usually. Whether you select a DJ or band, finalize arrangements at least six months prior to your wedding.

Live Bands

Assuming you can find a charismatic, golden-throated singer backed by talented, enthusiastic musicians, a live band is great. If you're lucky enough to find live musicians who can work within your budget, snap them up quickly—before another bride hires *your* band for *her* wedding.

If you're not so lucky, plan to spread yourself pretty thin. You're going to have to make many treks to bars, lounges, and function halls—anyplace where you might find some decent live music. Despite what your parents or anyone else says, be honest with yourself. Do you have the time and patience to see this search through? If you do find a group who strikes your fancy, listen to them perform a few times. With a one-shot deal, you have no idea whether you're hearing them on an especially good (and lucky) night, or whether they *always* sound like they should be on the radio.

Also make sure any band you consider comes with a wide range of musical styles and tempos in their repertoire. Do they have a really rigid style or do they know how to vary the pace? Are they relaxed and natural when they play—or do they look like they're having about as much fun as when they sit in the dentist's chair?

NAIL 'EM DOWN

Once you find your magic musical combo, give the band a list of songs you absolutely want played at your reception. If they don't know the songs already, will the band consider learning them in time? Ask about their sound system and equipment needs. If your reception site is too small, or doesn't have the proper electrical outlets and fuse power, it's better to know before you hire the band.

At most weddings, the bandleader doubles as the master of ceremonies. If you want your bandleader to perform this duty, find out whether he or she will be willing, and if any extra cost is involved.

Budget Boosters: Music

- *Negotiate a band's fee. If your wedding is the last Saturday in January, you'll have a lot more bargaining power than if it's the last Saturday in June. A band would almost always rather book a gig that pays a little less than have no gig at all.*

- *If your heart is set on a certain ten-member band, see if they play gigs with fewer members at a lower price.*

- *Contract your band to play for fewer hours, and you'll cut down on the cost. You can play CDs during the dinner hour.*

GET IT IN WRITING

Before you sign a contract with the band, make sure you've stipulated the following points in writing:

- **The band's attire:** You don't want them showing up at a formal wedding in ripped jeans and gym shorts.
- **The band's arrival time:** Make sure the band is set up with instruments tuned before the guests arrive. The band's sound check will probably not make for soothing dinner music.
- **The exact cost of hiring the band:** . . . and everything included for that price. Some bands charge you if they have to add an extra piece of equipment; others charge a fee for playing requests, still others charge overtime by the hour.

Disc Jockeys

Some people insist live bands are "classier" than disc jockeys, but not if they're horrible musicians. Because it can be so difficult to find a *really good* band, disc jockeys are fast becoming the wedding music option of choice. A DJ is perfectly acceptable at a semiformal or formal wedding. They're considerably less expensive than a band. But they have other benefits, too: They give you the original version of a song, so you have no worries about sketchy renditions of your favorites, and they're less of a logistical headache. They can also provide more song variety than a band. These days, really sharp DJs come equipped with a full load of MP3s, so guests can request almost anything at the reception.

It's just as important to see and hear a disc jockey in action as it is with a band. When interviewing DJs, look for the same things: balance, variety, a good mix of fast and slow songs, a good personality, and first-rate equipment. Pay attention to the DJ's mannerisms—does he talk way too much or far too little? The best DJs excel as master of ceremonies, flawlessly flowing dinner music to dancing, and parents' dances to cake cutting.

Find out how big his or her music collection is; your disc jockey should be able to accommodate the majority of your guests' requests. Provide a list of what you want played at the reception (and if you have some songs you absolutely, positively, upon penalty of death *do not* want played, give him a hit list of those, too!). Some other questions to ask your DJ:

◆ How many weddings has he provided music for? What size weddings does he typically work?

◆ Will he provide appropriate music for the cocktail hour?

◆ If some of the music you want isn't available, is the DJ willing to purchase it?

◆ Does he provide a wireless microphone for any toasts or speeches?

◆ Is gratuity included in the price?

The DJ's exact costs, the time of arrival and departure, the place, and his proper attire should also be included in your contract.

The Songs

Your choices for reception music are limited only by your imagination. The only guideline you should be aware of is that you want to entertain your guests—not drive them away.

Aside from pleasing the guests, you and your fiancé should make sure your own favorite music is played during the reception. What good is it if you play lots of music to please the older crowd, but you don't want to dance?

Your best bet is to go with an all-inclusive song list that covers a broad spectrum of musical tastes—some slow, some dance tunes, some rock, some soul.

Poised Under Pressure: **Dance with Both Dads**

If your parents are divorced and remarried, and you are particularly close with your stepfather, there's no need to leave anyone out. Why not choose to have two father-daughter dances?

If you feel particularly ambitious, poll your family and friends for suggestions, and then compile an eclectic playlist that's guaranteed to please everybody.

Helpful hint: Find out in advance where the speakers will be located in you reception room, then seat your older guests away from them—and away from where the musicians will be playing. This should prevent complaints from your elderly relatives about the excessive loudness of the music.

DJ/Bandleader To-Do List

As soon as your reception gets started, things will move quickly. You don't want to get tripped up with what happens when or who's doing what. The best way to ensure that things flow smoothly is by going over all of the details in advance with your DJ or bandleader. Remember, as emcee, this person will be responsible for introducing the appropriate people and events at your reception. Consider the following possibilities:

◆ Will your DJ/bandleader introduce just you and your groom or the entire bridal party? What about parents, grandparents, or other important family members?

◆ What about music for the introductions? Discuss your options—often, a band or DJ will play different music selections for the parents and grandparents, wedding party, and bride and groom as they enter the reception.

◆ Be sure your DJ/bandleader has all of the names (and the proper pronunciations) for everyone being introduced:

Parent(s) of bride

Parent(s) of groom

Grandparent(s) of bride

Grandparent(s) of groom

Flower girl(s) and ringbearer(s)

Bridesmaids and ushers (paired up accordingly)

Maid/matron of honor

Best man

Bride and groom as they are to be introduced. (If, for example, you are not changing your maiden name, be sure your DJ/bandleader is aware of that.)

◆ Is there going to be a blessing before dinner? If so, by whom?

◆ Who is giving the first toast? Who will follow with additional toasts, and in what order?

◆ Will anyone join you in your first dance? Will you have an additional dance right after your first dance with your wedding party?

◆ What other special dances would you like to fit in?

◆ Do you have a certain song in mind for your cake cutting?

◆ Will you be having a bouquet and garter toss, or do you prefer to do something different, such as an anniversary dance?

◆ Do you have other song requests, such as ethnic dances? Are there elements you want to avoid, such as line dances, congas, and so on?

◆ Do you want to play any special songs for other people at your wedding? For instance, announcing and playing your parents' and grandparents' wedding songs is a nice sentimental touch.

◆ What song would you like to be played for your last dance?

Classic Rewind

Music can make or break any party—especially a wedding. Invest enough time and effort into this important element, and your wedding will be a success. As long as your DJ or band does a good job, plays a fair mix of musical styles, and gets your guests out on the dance floor, everyone will enjoy themselves. Don't worry if a few people don't like certain songs or grumble because they've never heard them before—most guests will get into the groove. The important thing is that songs reflect your personalities—and your true sentiments about the people for whom they're chosen.

Music Notes

Photography

Once it's lights, camera, action for your big day, you want to be sure you've enlisted a reliable photographer to capture the special moments. Yes, photographers can be expensive, but remember, those pictures are what you'll have left to relive your wedding day. Don't cut corners here. Ask around, do the research, and talk to several people to get a feel for different photographic styles. Even if someone you like isn't available on your day, good photographers will refer you to other good photographers, so start networking!

Don't Cut Corners!

Because you're probably shelling out loads of money for your wedding, it's tempting to cut corners. That might be okay in certain areas, but photography is *not* one of them. Professional photographers don't come cheap because there's much more to good photography than a simple aim, auto-focus, and shoot routine. It's an art, and it requires skill and planning.

Imagine how you'll feel if your photos come back blurry or ill-composed, contain colors that don't appear in nature, or feature shots of family and friends with demonic red dots in their eyes. Now you know why it pays to be careful with this decision.

GOING RATES

Until you sit down with a photographer to hash out the battle plan for your wedding, you'll probably be dealing with price ranges rather than concrete amounts. The final price will depend on the approach to the wedding you develop together. Go ahead and look for the best value, but remember: You'll do yourself a big favor paying a little more for a quality job.

Captured on Film

The best wedding photographers catch lots of candid, special moments, yet you barely know they're there. If you're expecting a wedding album filled with shot after shot of posed pictures, think again. You *can* go this traditional route; just realize that there are more and more pros these days who take a creative approach to their work, and it makes a difference.

Look for a photographer whose style suits your taste. You're going to be spending a lot of time with this individual as you take tons of pictures. Make sure you feel comfortable and at ease with your photographer, because your mood and expression will show in your photos!

PHOTOJOURNALISTS

The photojournalistic style is becoming increasingly popular for wedding photography. Photojournalists aim to catch their subjects in the moment,

Budget Boosters: Photography and Videography

- *The closer in line your ceremony and reception are time wise, the less you'll have to worry about overtime expenses. Or, if there is a significant lapse between ceremony and reception, and your photographer's studio is nearby, see if you can negotiate a break in the services.*

- *If possible, wait to order your final album and prints until you have the funds to do so after the wedding.*

- *Cut video costs by purchasing an unedited package—this will minimize the videographer's time-consuming task of cutting, editing, and adding background music. Or, if you really want a nicely edited video, go for a basic package, and omit all the costly special effects.*

with lots of candid and unstructured shots. Photojournalists capture the spontaneous expressions and smaller details that traditional wedding photographers gloss over while busy posing you. The results are priceless, as real emotions of joy, surprise, melancholy, and contentment are caught on film forever. It's also a great style to use if you don't have the patience to pose for a lot of photos. Good photojournalists are sure to pose couples for some formal portraits, and then also take a wealth of unstructured shots.

LAID OUT IN BLACK AND WHITE

Black-and-white adds an artistic, timeless quality to photos. Your photographer can give black-and-white prints a sepia tone—that antique, golden glow of old photos—or focus on a small but integral portion of a black-and-white photo, such as the bridal bouquet, boutonniere, centerpieces, or cake flowers, and tint them with color. Mix any of these options in with typical color shots and, suddenly, your photos have a more interesting range of depth, mood, and tone.

Going Digital

If you're a gadget-crazed girl (or you're marrying a gadget-crazed guy), you probably wondered immediately what your digital photography options might be. Although the newest way might always seem like the best way, don't be so quick to judge.

Classic Concerns: **Proofs and Negatives Included**

Plenty of traditional photographers still insist on charging extra for the proofs and retaining your negatives. With these types, it's all about paying for the number of photos you get. It's wiser—and ultimately more cost-efficient—to enlist the services of a photographer who includes all of the proofs and negatives in the total package cost. This way, you can be sure you are paying for creativity and talent, not reprint fees!

Classic Concerns: Be Candid

Talk to your photographer ahead of time about taking plenty of candid photos. Otherwise, you'll end up with a bunch of posed photos you aren't especially happy with because they don't capture the real feeling of your wedding.

Digital pictures do have their advantages. Generally speaking, digital wedding packages are often slightly cheaper. You might end up with more pictures, but this is not necessarily so. Digital pictures can easily be put onto a CD-ROM so that you can e-mail them to friends and family. You can also have them put onto a DVD. Having the pictures on a CD is also the equivalent of having the negatives; you can make all the copies you want.

The downside of most digital photos is that as you enlarge them, you lose clarity and they often end up blurred. If you can live with that, digital may be something worth looking into. Some photographers offer a combination of traditional film and digital.

Calling All Photographers

Finding the right professional might not be a walk in the park. It's common for the best people to be booked a year or more in advance, so be prepared to start your search early. Don't flip if the first person a friend recommends is booked—remember, good photographers know other good photographers, and they will be happy to refer you accordingly.

PERSONALITY TEST

If you're relying on word-of-mouth advice, make sure to ask people not only about the quality of their photos, but also their impressions of the overall experience with the photographer or studio in question. Their pictures might be a dream, while their experience was a nightmare. If so, keep looking.

Remember, you're looking for someone who makes you feel comfortable, someone who is willing to work with you every step of the way, on *your* terms, not someone who pushes you around and attempts to dictate the vision of your day.

THE EX(PERIENCE) FACTOR

How can you be sure you've found someone who knows what he or she is doing? Pay attention to details when you look at samples:

- Look for good color, crispness, and well-balanced composition in all shots.
- Be sure the photographer makes good use of lighting.
- Pay attention to the variety of backgrounds and settings used. (You don't want an album full of wedding shots where everyone is standing in the same place.)
- Consider whether there's sufficient balance between formal and candid shots.

When you're interviewing potential photographers (especially those you've cold-called without knowing much about)—ask for references. The photos in the portfolio he's showing you might look incredible, but you have no way of knowing how much this guy has self-edited his selection.

Sizing Them Up

You'll need to ask a lot of questions to find the right photographer. Here, more than ever, your gut instincts mean a lot. If anything about a potential candidate makes you feel you can't trust this person to do the job correctly, move on. There are plenty of other photographers out there.

THE RIGHT QUESTIONS

Don't be afraid to put your photographer through the wringer. Long after you've stored away your wedding gown and dried the bouquet you carried, you and your loved ones will go back to your wedding photographs time and again. Find out *before* you sign a contract exactly what you're getting into:

- How long has he or she been in business? Does he or she specialize in weddings? Is he or she a full-time photographer?
- What kinds of packages does he or she offer? What's included in each package? What are the costs for additional photos?
- Does a mix of black-and-white and color photos cost more?
- How many pictures does he or she typically take at a wedding?
- Is there an hourly fee, or a fee for travel? What about overtime?
- Will you get all of your proofs and negatives as part of your package, or will you have to purchase additional, individual pictures?
- Are any albums, frames, and special parents' books included?
- Can you see some of his or her recent work and have the names of some former clients as references?

THE ANSWERS YOU SEEK

Since most people don't have a lot of experience working with professional photographers on such a grand scale, you might not be sure about the answers you should expect. Here's what to watch for when you interview candidates.

Classic Concerns: Your Shot List

Your photographer, no matter how exceptional, is not a mind reader. Give him a list of all of the special people you want included in the pictures, particularly anyone who isn't in the wedding party. Then be sure to ask someone close to you who knows all of your family and friends to direct the photographer to the appropriate individuals on the day of the wedding.

Steer clear of part-time photographers who only handle weddings occasionally. You want a full-time photographer; not someone who takes photos as a hobby, or someone who uses photography to make a little extra money on the side.

Avoid large studios that use the assembly-line approach. These types often employ as many as 100 photographers and won't guarantee which one will show up on your wedding day, or how qualified he or she is to do the job. If the studio you choose employs several photographers, always ask to see sample photos taken by the photographer who'll shoot your wedding. If this studio can't or won't supply them, find another photographer.

If you're planning to work with a studio, choose one that specializes in weddings. You might love the studio that did your high school graduation pictures, but if portraits are all they do, they'll probably flunk out at your wedding. Experienced wedding photographers know how to avoid problems, when to fade into the background, and how to pull things together when working with a crowd.

Ask for prices up front. Complete fees for photographers can run thousands of dollars. Some photographers will quote you a package price based on your receiving a certain number of finished photos. (These are usually old school, traditional types; photographers who take a more contemporary approach will quote you a price for their time and then take many more photos.) Whatever the package specifics, a quality studio or photographer will take three times as many photos as you expect, to give you the best and broadest selection.

Poised Under Pressure: Take Formals First

You don't want to miss out on all the fun of your wedding because you're posing for pictures. Take all of the necessary shots before the reception.

Photography Notes

Videography

To video or not to video? That is the *other* question. Still photos can capture the atmosphere and emotion of a particular moment, but if you want to feel as if you can step right back into your wedding day at any time, or you really wish you could see the expression on your faces as you take your vows, you should consider hiring a videographer, too.

Captured on Video

Some couples have a hard time deciding whether or not to employ a videographer. This is understandable, since the service can tack on several thousand more dollars to your total wedding costs. Yet, many couples value their video just as much—or more—than their photos, because video shows them all the things that flew past them.

Unlike a still camera, the video camera records time as it's unfolding, taking in all the sound and action of a scene. Everyone will be watching you on that altar, but you and your groom won't get to see what that looks like—until you watch your video. Video captures *all* the guests at your wedding as they sing, dance, eat, kiss, cry, and laugh. When a bride and groom finally sit down to watch their video, it not only brings back old memories, it shows them new things they hadn't seen before.

Don't leave the videotaping to a friend or relative unless you've seen a sample of his or her work and were impressed by it. Your groom's brother might have the best intentions, but he'll probably miss some key moments while he's schmoozing and taking part in the festivities. And even if he

Poised Under Pressure: **Meet and Greet**

Make sure your videographer and photographer meet ahead of time if they haven't crossed paths at a wedding before yours. If your photographer and videographer get comfortable with each other ahead of time, they'll be more likely to work well together. Then you can rest easy.

Classic Concerns: **Double Up**

Sometimes you can get a cheaper deal by booking the same company for a photo/video combo rather than hiring a photographer and videographer separately. This will also help you to consolidate your efforts—you'll save time and the confusion of coordinating extra vendor meetings.

owns a good video camera, odds are he won't have the necessary sound and editing equipment to make a tape for posterity.

Interviewing Your Videographer

When searching for a videographer, apply the same basic guidelines you would for a still photographer. The images should be crisp and clear, and colors should be true-to-life. You want to be comfortable with your videographer and confident he won't be ordering your guests in and out of shots because he fancies himself the next Big Man on the Hollywood Scene.

Here are some important points to consider:

♦ Does he or she have up-to-date, quality equipment?

♦ How long has he or she been doing this professionally?

♦ What type of editing and dubbing capabilities will be used?

♦ Will you and your groom be wearing microphones during the ceremony?

♦ How many cameras does he or she have?

♦ How many people will be assisting on the job? (Some video formats require the simultaneous use of two cameras.)

♦ Can you view sample tapes? (Watch for smooth editing, clear sound, and an overall professional look and feel to the tape.)

♦ What kinds of packages does he or she offer? What are the rates? Are there any extra fees? (Ask about travel expenses, hourly rates, overtime fees, and so on.)

- What formats does he or she offer? Can you have a DVD instead of a VHS tape (or vice versa)? What is the price difference?
- Can you have several copies made? What will extra copies cost?
- Does he or she add any special editing or musical effects?
- Can you get the names of former clients for references?

There's plenty of great technology available these days. You don't have to settle for anything short of broadcast-quality production values.

SAMPLE CONSIDERATIONS

When you're viewing samples of a videographer's work, consider whether the segments tell a story. You should get a feel for the actual progression of a wedding day when you watch a video. The "big events" at the ceremony and reception, such as the vows and ring exchange, the introduction of the wedding party, the cake cutting, and so on, should be clearly highlighted.

You can sign up for all sorts of extras—but those services won't come cheap. Before you get carried away, remember that little technicality called your budget. You don't necessarily need all the frills; determine which basic or additional features are *most important* to you.

Video Techniques

As with photographers, package prices and options vary greatly. Many videographers will give you a choice of extra editing elements, such as

Classic Concerns: **Get the Master Copy**

Whether your videographer gives you VHS or DVD copies, be sure to ask for your master tape. Not only will this give you the entire footage from your wedding, it's like having your photo negatives. Just in case your tapes or DVDs ever get ruined, you'll have a backup.

Location Scouting

Whatever you decide in the photo and video departments, remember to take your photographer and videographer to your ceremony and reception sites ahead of time to check out the lighting, possible angles, and so on. Some couples choose to shoot photos and video footage at an additional location, such as a beach or garden. If you plan to take your photo shoot on the road, scout it out with your photographer and videographer well in advance. This way, you can investigate whether you need any special permits or permission to use the area.

including the names of the bridal party on your video and selecting background music. Beyond that, talk to your videographer about the flow and pace of your video, since his or her creative vision will ultimately drive the final result. Asking about certain styles will help you to understand your videography options better.

Note: Lots of couples—and videographers—think it's a great idea to roam the reception requiring every guest to give a recorded comment. Sure, it's nice to capture your guests' sentiments on video, but not at the expense of their comfort. A smarter strategy is setting up a special "video station" in a particular location, so that guests can speak directly to the camera if and when they choose. You'll get lots of well-thought-out private footage, without putting your guests on the spot.

A straight-shot format uses only one camera. It's the least expensive video option because no editing is used, but the videographer can still add small touches, such as names and dates, to help liven up the film.

A nostalgic format usually starts with a photomontage of you and your groom as children and young adults, and then moves to photos that show the two of you together. You'll have to round up some cute pictures from your childhood for this. You'll also give your videographer copies of your wedding invitation, program, favors, and any other wedding-day items. From there, the video will follow the events of your ceremony and reception.

A documentary format usually begins with you and your groom preparing for the ceremony, then proceeds to scenes of the wedding and the reception; sometimes interviews with family and friends are added, too.

Because the second and third options require more work, they can be more expensive. Prices vary widely depending on the type of equipment used, the number of locations included, the length of time for which the videographer is contracted, and the amount of editing required.

Very important hint: Make sure your photographer and videographer know exactly how to spell your name, your groom's name, and the names of any members of your wedding party. If you don't provide correct spellings from the start, they might end up wrong on the cover of your wedding album or in the listing of your bridal party on your video!

Classic Rewind

In the case of either photography or video, discuss when you want to get things started on your wedding day. Do you want your photographer or videographer to shoot you getting ready at your parents house, or will they arrive at the ceremony, for example? These decisions will affect the final price of your package. Many photographer's and videographer's charges are based on a set number of hours. If yours offer eight-hour packages, but your wedding will require nine or ten hours of shooting, work out overtime issues in advance.

Whatever you decide with your photography and videography, reserve an ample slice of your budget for these services. Don't sell yourselves or your day short by taking what you think is the cheap or easy way out, only to have your hopes dashed when your photos and video don't measure up.

Videography Notes

Classic Style

Here's where you'll find savvy strategies on choosing great dresses, tuxedos, and accessories for you and your wedding party. Who wears what, and how do you zero in on your look and keep the process simple? There are many tricks to streamlining these details.

It probably goes without saying that as soon as you're engaged you'll be jazzed about starting your search for the perfect gown. But don't forget to start looking for your bridesmaids' dresses well in advance. You'll need enough time to have their dresses made or ordered, and altered. You can afford to wait a little longer with the men because, as usual, getting them primped and polished for the big day is a lot easier. Once you rent their tuxedos, with a few stitches here and there, they'll be ready to go.

The Beautiful Bride

In some ways, shopping for the perfect wedding dress is a lot like searching for the perfect guy: You might have to sort through a lot of losers before you find your winner. You thought choosing a bathing suit was tough? Just imagine the pressure you'll put on yourself to find the perfect wedding gown. Before you get started, do a little homework: Know what you're willing to pay for a gown; know the general style you're looking for; and know that not every dress shop is looking out for your best interests.

En Vogue?

Use magazines and Web sites to give you ideas for your wedding dress, but don't be a slave to the latest fashions! Just because you see a certain gown style splashed all over the place, that doesn't mean it's right for you. Besides, a good wedding dress design should be timeless—not trendy.

STYLE GUIDELINES

Before you start your search, consider the formality and time of day for your wedding. When buying a gown, your major considerations will be:

◆ **Fabric:** While many fabrics work for warm and cold weather, save heavy fabrics like velvet for winter weddings, and very light ones like chiffon for spring and summer.

◆ **Sleeves:** Can you wear a sleeveless gown in the coldest months? Sure—just bring along a formal wrap. Likewise, if you want to wear long sleeves in July, feel free. Consider your general comfort level, because an uncomfortable bride is never a happy one!

◆ **Length:** If you're having an informal ceremony, a dressy suit is certainly fine. If you're having an ultraformal wedding, a floor-length dress with a long train might be in order. For a semiformal wedding, you can go either tea length or floor length.

The most important thing is that your gown fits in with the overall style of your wedding and looks good on you.

TRAIN!

When talking trains, there are two things you'll want to keep in mind: length and style. Here are some common styles:

◆ **The sweep train** just touches (or *sweeps*) the floor.

◆ **The chapel train** trails three to four feet behind your gown.

◆ **The cathedral (or monarch) train** ranges from six to eight feet long and trails behind you.

◆ **The royal cathedral train** trails ten (or more) feet behind you.

◆ **The watteau train** is a unique alternative that falls from the shoulder blades to the hem of the gown.

> ## *Poised Under Pressure:* Don't Go It Alone
>
> *It's wise to take at least one person along on your gown-shopping excursion—to help you sort through style options and to baby you when you're frustrated because you can't find the right one. Don't take more than a few people with you, however. The situation can be stressful enough without listening to the conflicting opinions of five other people!*

Let the Games Begin!

Wedding gowns can take six months or longer to arrive after the order is placed, so start making your way through the racks of satin, silk, taffeta, chiffon, brocade, shantung, and organza right away.

Some brides try on one or two dresses and make a decision, while others go through fifty or more before the right one comes along. Be patient, and don't get discouraged—eventually, you'll find the right dress, and when you do, you'll just *know*.

BRIDAL SALONS

Most salons require an appointment; you can usually get one with a few days' notice. Making appointments is worth the trouble, as it ensures that the staff will give you the proper attention. Don't be surprised if you feel like Cinderella being fitted for her magic slipper. Salon employees are hoping their lavish treatment will translate directly into lavish amounts of money spent. Be careful: Smiles, compliments, and free coffee, tea, and champagne do not necessarily ensure quality dresses or reputable business practices.

Buyer Beware

Unfortunately, some bridal shops will try to milk you for as much money as they possibly can, while, in exchange, they provide little quality. Be informed of some of the more common schemes. The majority of salons require a deposit equal to half the price of the dress. Rather than order your dress right away, they'll hold your deposit and use the money for other things (like earning interest in the company checking account). Then they order your gown at the last minute, which means it might not be ready in time.

Get every aspect of your gown's purchase in writing, including the delivery date. Find out the store's policy regarding late or damaged gowns and ask about when, exactly, the shop plans to order your dress. Call periodically to check on progress. If (God forbid) something should go seriously wrong, don't be afraid to take legal action—or at least to threaten it. You may be surprised at the action you'll see once the word *lawyer* enters the conversation.

Bridal Bargains

So you're a real bargain shopper? Hope you have some mettle—looking for bargain bridal dresses is hard work. For every bride who finds the dress of her dreams at a fraction of the price, there are ten others who have nothing but frustration to show for their bargain hunting.

Hit the Sales

If you want a great wedding dress but you're watching your budget, keep your eyes peeled for sample sales and clearance events. You can find designer dresses you've drooled over in bridal magazines at significant savings, but it's hit or miss. What you see is what you get—you usually can't order special sizes and must purchase your dress off the rack.

Of course, the mere thought of finding a dress for as little as $100 drives lots of women nuts, so be prepared for a madhouse if you brave this option. You'll still have to hustle to find a seamstress to do the alterations, which won't come cheap. And it goes without saying that you won't get the pampering of a bridal salon; you'll be lucky to get space at the mirror!

USED/CONSIGNMENT GOWNS

If you're not the sentimental type, purchasing a preowned dress might work for you. Just be honest with yourself and make sure you're okay with wearing a wedding dress someone you don't know has worn before. Finding a quality wedding gown on consignment may require tenacity; they don't come down the pike every day. Check the classified section of the local newspaper, visit nicer consignment shops, and talk to shop owners.

The downside to purchasing a previously worn gown: Bridal salons may not do alterations on gowns that are not bought at their store, so you'll have to search for a reliable seamstress. Be forewarned: Talented seamstresses are few and far between. And, unfortunately, the expense of these alterations *may* nullify the money you saved.

OTHER THRIFTY OPTIONS

You might instead ask your mother or grandmother to pull out her wedding dress. If it's not exactly your style or size, have a seamstress or tailor update it to reflect your taste. Another creative way to save money on your bridal gown is to buy a bridesmaid's dress in white. These are usually much less expensive than the average wedding dress.

The Bridesmaids' Dresses

If you've bought countless style-challenged dresses for your girlfriends' weddings, you probably feel like now it's payback time. However, consider taking the higher ground. Deciding whether the party should dress formally or casually is the easy part; the type of wedding you're planning will dictate that. Now you just need to settle on something everybody looks good in—and likes.

COLOR YOUR WEDDING

Your wedding colors should be colors you *really* like, as you'll be seeing them on your bridesmaids, your flowers, your wedding favors, your decorations, and even your cake. If you have a couple of favorites that go well together, choose both. Just be sure they don't clash!

Some people operate by the old seasonal conventions that dictate cool pastel shades such as pale pink or ice blue for warm-weather weddings and deep, rich colors such as forest green or burgundy for weddings during the cooler months. This does not necessarily have to be the case. Imagine you're looking at your wedding photos. Do you want the bridesmaids' dresses to blend in subtly? If so, go for a lighter shade. However, if contrast is what you're looking for with your wedding, a deeper shade will be more of a complement against a white or off-white gown.

DRESS TO IMPRESS

As the bride, you can select whatever dress you like, but if it doesn't look good on *all* of your bridesmaids, ultimately, it won't bode well for the wedding. You want everyone to feel confident and gorgeous on your wedding day—obviously because their happiness and comfort level matter to you, but also because it will have a tremendous impact on the overall look of your wedding. Don't forget that you'll be seeing those dresses—and the way your bridesmaids look in them—for years to come in your photos and video. There's a lot riding on this, so choose wisely!

COLLECTIVE INPUT

It's always smart to involve bridesmaids in the dress selection. If you know you can trust your bridesmaids to keep an open mind and cooperate, bring them along for the search. Narrow it down to a few top choices, then e-mail the style numbers for each dress to anyone who couldn't make it. Let everyone vote on the top choice and go with the general consensus. Above all else, do whatever you can to decide on a dress that *everyone* finds acceptable. You don't want *anyone* to feel awkward or unattractive.

Classic Concerns: **Order All Dresses Together**

Never have your bridesmaids order their dresses at separate bridal salons. Aside from saving you headaches keeping track of who ordered what where, this will ensure that all of the dresses come from the same dye lot.

Traditionally, the members of the bridal party wear the same style dress, but you shouldn't be afraid of variety. If you really want to make your bridesmaids happy, simply select a certain color and style, then allow each one to select a dress that looks best on her.

You'll make your life easiest and least complicated if you order your bridesmaids dresses through the bridal salon where you get your gown. If, however, you're looking to find dresses that are less expensive, check out the formal dress sections of quality department stores in your area.

The Perils of Alterations

Alterations are one of life's necessary evils. You want the dresses for your wedding to look perfect, after all. But all those little nips and tucks can cost a fortune. There are several ways to protect your bridesmaids and yourself from getting raked over the coals in this department.

Some salons make a standard practice of advising women to order dresses in a size much larger than normally necessary. The usual excuse is that the dresses "run really small." Too often, however, the *real* reason is so that the shop can make a bundle off of the alterations.

Take matters into your own hands. If the dress you're considering has a tag in it, and the dress seems to fit just fine, order that size. If the tag has been removed, or it's not the right size, try on other dresses from the same maker until you can settle on a size that closely approximates the right fit.

No one in your wedding party will be pleased to save $50 on a dress, only to get charged $45 for a hem, $35 to take in the waist, $25 to raise the dress straps, and so on! Look for a shop that includes a set fee for alterations.

On the other hand, if you have a bridesmaid who insists she's going to lose fifteen pounds before your wedding, try to convince her to order a dress that suits her present body shape. Most smart dressmakers leave room for slight weight fluctuations when ordering a dress, but even the best seamstresses have their limitations.

Once everyone has ordered their dresses, they should all set up alterations at their own convenience; just be sure to give them a deadline for getting that done. If one of your bridesmaids lives far away and can't make it to town for the fittings, send it to her so she can have alterations done at a bridal salon in her city.

A word to the wise—do yourself a favor: Build in a space cushion by telling your salon your wedding will take place a week earlier than it will in actuality. This way, if anything goes wrong at the last minute, you'll be covered.

Dressing the Men

Most men rent formalwear for a wedding. As long as a groom knows the wedding basics—formality level, season, time of day—just about any formalwear shop can point him (and his attendants) in the right direction. As mentioned in Part 1, your groom should start scouting out his wedding ensemble at least three to four months before the big day; the groomsmen should reserve theirs as soon as your groom makes his decision. For a formal wedding, the fathers of the bride and groom should wear a tuxedo style that works well with that of the attendants.

Classic Concerns: Footwear Freedom

Just as general body types vary, so do feet. What works for one bridesmaid might be incredibly uncomfortable for another! Let your bridesmaids choose their own shoes!

While your groom and his attendants might think it's a great idea to wear three-button suits with long ties, the older gents in the wedding party, like the fathers and grandfathers, might not necessarily agree. There's no reason why all the men should look like carbon copies of each other. If Dad is game, but Grandpa's more comfortable in something else, go for it.

If any of your male attendants live out of town, ask them to go to a reputable tuxedo shop to be measured. Then have them call in their measurements so you can reserve all of the attire at once, from one location.

Know Your Measurements

When it comes to measurements, women are used to the magic three—bust, waist, hips. There's a bit more involved with the guys' measurements, however. Be sure to pass on the correct information, so they don't botch this:

Measurements

Height:_____ Weight: _____

Tuxedo style and color: _____

Coat size: _____

Arm inseam: _____

Pants waist:_____

Length (outseam): _____

Shirt neck: _____

Sleeve length: _____

Shoe Size:_____ Shoe Width: _____

Classic Concerns: **Be Precise**

Remember to ask your formalwear shop about exact prices, including shoe rentals and any other accessories. Don't forget alterations—just because you're renting, that doesn't mean those fees don't apply. Also inquire about the shop's tuxedo return policy and the time of return.

The Younger Crowd

A junior bridesmaid can wear the same dress as the other bridesmaids, or a different style that is appropriate to her age. Flower girls can wear either long or short dresses that match or complement the other dresses. If you have a hard time finding something appropriate, don't fret; a white dress trimmed with lace or fabric that matches the other dresses is always a great option.Ringbearers and male pages can dress exactly as the other men in the party, or they can wear dress shorts or knickers.

All the Extras

Sure, finding the perfect dress is cause for celebration—but you're not done yet. You still need a veil, a headpiece, shoes, jewelry, and any other items that will complete your ensemble. Gather your strength and pick yourself up off the couch—you're heading back into the trenches.

WHERE'S YOUR HEAD?

Your headpiece and veil should *complement* your dress, not overpower it. Don't pick something ridiculously elaborate. Remember, you want all eyes focused on you—the complete package—not a little body and tiny head hidden under a massive headpiece.

Although a headpiece usually takes only eight to ten weeks to arrive after you order it, try to order it before that. Having the headpiece in advance gives you enough time to pull your look together and go through one or two trial runs with your hairdresser.

Poised Under Pressure: **Don't Go Match Crazy**

You and your groom should be a perfect match, but the same doesn't neces-sarily hold true when it comes to your mothers' dresses. This is a day for both of your mothers to shine. You want them to feel as comfortable and confi-dent as possible. Barring any awful color clashes or distasteful displays, give the moms some freedom of choice here!

YOUR PURSE

You naturally won't come strolling down the aisle purse in hand, but you will need a bag to carry your personal items—lipstick, mirror, hairbrush, tissues for tears of joy. Your purse should obviously go with your ensemble. Some dressmakers will even make you a cute little drawstring bridal bag from fabric that matches or complements your dress.

FANCY FOOTWORK

Silk or satin has always been the rule of thumb for wedding shoes, but no one says you have to go for the standard, boring pump. In the summer, a fancy pair of sandals is perfectly acceptable. One word of warning—all whites are *not* the same. Bring along a small swatch of your dress when searching for shoes.

Although it's always tempting to choose fashion over function, when it comes to wedding shoes, choosing a pair you can dance and stand in com-fortably is your first priority. Break your shoes in before the wedding, and if you're wearing high heels, bring along a pair of comfy flats for later.

DON'T GET HOSED

When it comes to hose, avoid opaque white stockings. Sheer stockings look classier and are more flattering. Go for the sheerest champagne, nude, or pale blush color you can find. Sheer white or ivory is fine, too. Have an extra pair handy on the big day in case you get an unexpected run.

What if you're getting married in the summer and you don't want to wear stockings? Although some would argue it's not appropriate for a bride to go stockingless, if you're wearing a full-length gown, don't worry. Modesty *is not* an issue here. Break out a great pair of dressy sandals, sport a sparkly toe ring, and you're set.

Underneath It All

One very important distinction when it comes to choosing your gown: Do you want a large, full skirt, or a streamlined straight or A-line style? If the former is what you have in mind, be prepared to don lots of layers. (Beware: Big puffy dresses can get *really* heavy.) But maybe the Scarlett O'Hara look just isn't for you. In that case, be mindful of the gowns you try. You can't just remove all of the petticoats if you don't want them. Certain gowns are designed to fall a certain way. If you want a streamlined look, point that out to salon attendants, and ask them to bring you only straight or A-line styles.

Note: Don't forget any special undergarments, such as a strapless or pushup bra, a corset, tummy reducing underwear, stockings, and a slip. Although salons offer these items, they're often overpriced. You're better off buying them elsewhere.

Classic Rewind

When it comes to decking everyone out for your wedding, streamlining the apparel process cannot be stressed enough. If at all possible, go through the same bridal/formalwear shop for all of your dresses and tuxedos. You'll save yourself a lot of running around and coordinating at the eleventh hour.

Dress, Tux, and Accessory Notes

Flowers

Whether you're going for monotone elegance or bright contrast, beautiful fresh flowers can have a powerful impact on the look of your wedding. They can also cost a pretty penny. This is no time for shrinking violets—if you're going to pay the price, they'd better have some pizzazz. You might think you're done in the floral department once you choose bouquets for you and the maids, plus boutonnieres for your guy and his groomsmen, but hold on. You've still got parents, grandparents, godparents, special relatives, and other ceremony participants to think about. Not to mention decorations for your ceremony site and centerpieces at the reception. There are many ways to include fresh flowers in the festivities, and you can come up with other unique alternatives, too.

Finding Your Florist

Depending on what you select, flower prices vary. That's why it's important to start with a firm budget before you talk to any florists. An honest florist, when presented with a set-in-stone budget, will steer you in the most practical direction to get you the most bang for your buck. Once you settle on the budget, then you can move on to the fun part—choosing the actual flowers.

As usual, go on referrals. Be sure to ask for photos of previous displays the florist has done, and check references to determine the actual quality of the flowers. After you decide on a florist, you'll need a written contract stipulating costs, times, dates, places, and services.

Classic Concerns: **Your Flowers Await**

Make sure your florist is scheduled to arrive before *your photographer on your wedding day. You want to have your flowers in all of your photos; otherwise, you'll notice this conspicuous lack when you look through your albums later on!*

WHEN YOUR FLORIST TALKS, LISTEN

You might think all you need to do is stroll into a meeting with your florist, tell her exactly what you want, and then place your order. That might work if money's no option, but even so, there are other things to consider. A sharp florist will have plenty of advice to share when it comes to creating beautiful floral arrangements on a budget, shopping for flowers in season, making sure flowers don't wilt, and coordinating flower selections that will fit best with the overall look and décor of your wedding.

Your florist will guide you to the flowers that most suit your style and taste—and even your coloring. Your florist will also tell you which flowers will look best in the ceremony and reception locations you've chosen. If you're getting married in a huge cathedral, for example, you'll need more substantial pieces than if you're taking your vows in a teeny tiny chapel. If the florist has never done work at your wedding location, take a trip there together so you can look around and discuss what will be needed—and where.

Note: A good florist knows a bride's bouquet should be in proportion to her body! If you're tall and your stature can carry it, more power to you—order as big a bouquet as you'd like. But if you're petite, go with something that complements your size and doesn't hide your gown. Some florists will actually measure you and suggest a bouquet size that's just right.

FLORAL OPTIONS

Today, most florists stock fresh flowers that have been imported from Europe, the Middle East, South America, and other foreign regions, so that

Poised Under Pressure: **Valentine Flowers**

Planning a Valentine's Day wedding? Be prepared for your flowers to cost more than they would at another time of the year. Traditionally, orders that are set for delivery within the first two weeks of February are priced higher.

Budget Boosters: Flowers

- ◆ *Find a florist who'll work within your desired budget, rather than dictate a set service price.*

- ◆ *Choose less expensive blossoms—forgo roses for carnations. Or, if you really have your heart set on a certain type of flower, focus on using it in your bouquet and those of the bridesmaids, then go for simpler, less expensive blossoms if you need additional arrangements.*

- ◆ *Choose flowers that are local and in season. Everyone has a favorite flower, but you'd better face facts: If you love tulips and you're getting married in July, you'll pay a fortune to import them from another country. Beside the cost factor, tulips won't ever stand up to the heat.*

- ◆ *If you're really serious about cutting flower costs, go with informal bunches of wildflowers or even dried flowers.*

"in season" is no longer as much of an issue as it was in the past. All but a few of the most delicate flowers are available at any time of year—you'll just have to pay more for some of them if they have to be imported. Also, just because you *can* order a particular flower, doesn't mean you should. If your florist advises otherwise, because the flowers aren't hearty enough for a winter wedding or might wilt under the blistering summer sun, heed what she says. (If you do decide to take a chance on a particularly delicate or difficult-to-order flower, be sure to have a second choice as backup.)

Do It Yourself

All of this floral consultation might not be that important to you, and that's fine. You can go the no-frills route here and tackle the wedding flowers on your own. But first, here are some things you should know.

WHOLESALERS

One option is to find yourself a good wholesale dealer. If you don't know anyone who's ever dealt with a wholesale florist, look in the phone book, visit wedding fairs, and keep your eyes and ears open. Many wholesalers will whip up your arrangements and deliver the flowers to your church for a lower price than the fanciest flower shops.

Cyber Flowers

There are also plenty of Internet floral wholesalers who cater to thrifty, crafty brides. In addition to selling flowers at deep discounts, many Web sites offer instructional videos on how to arrange, tape, and wire your flowers. Some even provide e-mail support in case you have a trouble with your arrangements.

The upside to Internet flowers is that you stand to save a lot of money. The downside? It's a little risky. Though the flowers are shipped overnight and are refrigerated so that they arrive fresh on your doorstep on the morning of your wedding, there are still a lot of *what ifs* involved, as in: What if there's a storm and the plane carrying your flowers is grounded? What if you get the wrong flowers? What if the flowers arrive dead? There are no easy fixes to these predicaments.

The cyber flower option is not for the faint of heart. Unless you have nerves of steel, buy your flowers from someone in town. It will make your life easier.

Classic Concerns: Consult Your Color Swatch

Especially if you want colorful floral arrangements for your wedding day, coordinate the colors of your bridesmaids dresses with your florist. There are infinite shades of blue, purple, red, green, and so on; you don't want to clash. Bring a dress swatch to your florist, to give a good sense of what colors will complement nicely.

Flower Power

Carefully selected and arranged flowers add an artistic touch to any wedding, but did you know that a flower's beauty can be more than skin deep? Different types of flowers carry a meaning all their own. Choosing your blossoms based on their symbolism might make your wedding even more special. Be sure to include their meaning in your program so that all your guests will understand the relevance. Here's a rundown of different flowers and what they symbolize:

Amaryllis: Splendid beauty

Bachelor's Buttons: Celibacy or hope

Bluebell: Constancy

Buttercup: Riches

Calla lily: Beauty

Camellia: Perfect loveliness, gratitude

Carnation (pink):Boldness

Carnation (red): Pure, deep love

Carnation (white): Talent

Chrysanthemum: Wealth, abundance, truth

Daffodil: Regard

Daisy: Innocence, loyal love

Forget-me-not: True love

Freesia: Innocence

Gardenia: Purity, joy

Honeysuckle: generous, devoted, and genuine affection

Iris: Friendship

Hydrangea: Understanding

Ivy: Wedded love, fidelity

Jonquil: Affection returned

Lilac: Love's first emotions

Lily: Purity and innocence

Lily of the Valley: Completeness, happiness, contentedness

Lime: Conjugal bliss

Magnolia: Love of nature

Marigold: Sacred Affection

Myrtle: Love

Orange Blossom: Purity, loveliness

Orchid: Love

Rose: Love

Rose (white): Innocence and secrecy

Stephanotis: Happiness in marriage

Stock: Bonds of affection

Tulip: Perfect love; love declared

Ceremony Flowers

Flowers accent key points and create atmosphere at your ceremony. Some couples simply place one large or a few smaller arrangements around the altar, while others also place flowers on pews, windowsills, doors, and any other freestanding fixtures they can find. Be aware that some churches request you leave your ceremony flowers as a donation to the church, for parishioners to enjoy during services. In that case, you're best advised to keep things simple and inexpensive, and save your money for the flowers you'll take with you!

Solid Presentation

A good florist will know how to present flowers at your ceremony in ways that are creative, but not necessarily cost prohibitive. Simple flowers, when placed in decorative baskets, glass bowls, or vases, look lovely. Your florist could tie loose flowers and baby's breath into ribbon to decorate pews and chairs; wind ivy around railings; or choose potted flowers in season, such as lilies, tulips, daffodils, hyacinths, and poinsettias, to spruce up a church that needs a little extra flair.

Classic Concerns: Avoid Negative Connotations

With all of these flowers to choose from, you should be able to find something with the right symbolism for your bouquet. Just in case you're superstitious, though, you should know that historically, some flowers have carried negative symbolism as well. Lavender signifies distrust, yellow carnations represent disdain, and yellow roses stand for jealousy.

Creative Centerpieces

If your facility already provides the table centerpieces for your reception, you're in luck. Fresh floral centerpieces cost a hefty chunk of change—this necessity has been known to double the cost of some floral budgets! If you do have to come up with your own alternatives, don't worry—buy some inexpensive flowers and arrange them yourself.

There are plenty of other unique options. If you would like to use flowers, but you want them to look different than the standard large, centrally located centerpiece, try some of these ideas.

- **The individual touch:** Include small bud vases with a bloom at each place setting, which can also double as wedding favors.
- **More is better:** Instead of including one large arrangement at each guest table, place a cluster of smaller containers or vases in the center of the tables. Low blooms work best for a cluster effect, and once again, these can also double as wedding favors—one per couple.
- **Love in bloom:** Include a single bloom, such as a rose or tulip, tucked into each place card holder.
- **Wreath of flowers:** Ask your florist to design a wreath of flowers for table centers. Then, for some height, include candles or another item, such as tree ornaments at Christmastime.
- **Fruits and veggies:** Instead of—or in addition to—flowers, use other items in your centerpieces, such as lemons, limes, grapes, berries, pears, peaches, asparagus, gourds, zucchinis, and pumpkins.
- **Forgo symmetry:** You don't have to have twenty matching center-pieces for twenty matching tables. Mix it up by using similar blooms or a similar-colored flower in various containers.

If you use a lot of floral arrangements at your wedding, plan some mean-ingful ways to dispense them after the reception. You could give flowers to close friends or relatives, as a way of expressing your appreciation for their help during your wedding planning process. Or you could perhaps donate them to nursing homes or other charitable organizations.

NONFLORAL CENTERPIECES

There are also plenty of clever ways to create striking nonfloral centerpieces that are equally pretty and not so pricey:

- ◆ Group pillar candles together on a decorative glass plate or place taper candles in candelabras.

- ◆ Use helium balloon arrangements held down by decorative weights.

- ◆ Place tealights at each plate setting.

- ◆ Use large bowls filled with water and floating candles (or flower petals) on top.

- ◆ Use fish bowls filled with sand and shells, or anything else that relates to your wedding theme or the season.

- ◆ Include other items that match your theme, such as cowboy hats, miniature cars, and so on.

- ◆ Arrange other striking conversation pieces, such as Bonsai trees, small sculptures, or photo collages in beautiful frames (with different photos on each table).

Classic Concerns: Floral Road Trip

If your ceremony site doesn't grumble about removing your flowers, you should consider using those flowers at the reception as well to save money. Recruit a responsible friend or relative to transport the flowers from one place to the other and set them up before guests arrive. But first discuss your options with your reception facility's coordinator.

Classic Concerns: A Colorful Bridal Bouquet

There are those staunch traditionalists who insist that a bride should natu-rally carry white flowers down the aisle. If, however, the thought of all that white on white is enough to bore you to tears, consider a more colorful bou-quet. Colorful flowers can be quite beautiful against a white or off-white wedding gown. If you're not one who likes things to blend into the wood-work, go ahead and express your personality and don't be afraid to carry a bouquet that stands out.

BUY THE SUPPLIES YOURSELF

Instead of buying bowls, candleholders, or other centerpiece fixtures from a florist—who will mark up prices significantly—scout out local craft stores and other discount retailers for the items you need. Also keep in mind that your centerpieces don't have to match (for that matter, this can also apply to your favors). Antique-looking bowls, vases, candleholders, platters, or other items in different styles for each table can work as beautiful, creative accents. The important thing is to pick one item, and then look for varia-tions on that unifying theme.

Flower the People

Once you've set your floral scene, it's time to get down to the important business of which people need flowers for your wedding. Without further adieu, start planning:

- **Bouquets for the maids:** If you like, add something special to the maid-of-honor's flowers to set her off from the crowd.
- **The flower girl:** A basket of flowers or petals, or a small bouquet is fine.
- **The mothers, grandmothers, and godmothers:** They all receive spe-cial corsages just before the ceremony begins.

- **The men:** Your groom, groomsmen, fathers, grandfathers, godfathers, and ringbearer, if you have one, all need boutonnieres.

- **Other key players:** Consider including flowers for any other special relatives or ceremony participants. If your budget is wearing thin by this point, ask your florist to put together some simple arrangements with a single, long-stemmed flower surrounded by baby's breath or fern.

- **The toss bouquet:** Whether you're actually going to toss a bouquet or incorporate some other tradition here, you certainly don't want to throw the real thing. You'll need a smaller, less expensive arrangement for this purpose.

As you can see, there are lots of flowers to order for lots of people on your wedding day. If you're a savvy organized bride (and you must be by now, if you've read this information well) it's not likely you'll forget anyone. But just in case . . . ask your florist to come prepared with a few extra long-stemmed roses.

Classic Rewind

Fresh flowers seem so romantic and enticing that it's easy to get out of control and order up a storm. Some extra lilies here, some more roses there, and the next thing you know, your flower budget goes haywire. Have fun choosing your flowers, but be careful (and maybe even a little crafty) in this department. Focus your budget in the places that will matter most to you (and to your photos and video later on). Choose your flowers wisely—not based on whim alone—and you'll bring your pretty posies in on or even under budget, without sacrificing the ambience of your wedding.

Flower Notes

Transportation

Most couples want to arrive at their wedding in style, and these days there are more options than just the standard stretch limo. Innovative couples have been known to use anything and everything, including helicopters, boats, hot rods, antique cars, Harley-Davidsons, and even Lear jets, to get them to the church (and reception) on time. As long as something can move you from here to there, it's fair game. Admittedly, some of these options might seem more appealing than others; whatever you decide, start looking as soon as possible.

Luxe Limos

Limousines are the most common mode of wedding transportation. Though it might not be as original or exciting as, say, floating in on a hot-air balloon, a well-kept limousine has its perks. You can seat ten (or more) people comfortably, watch TV, serve yourself from the bar, and have a chauffeur at your beck and call.

ROOM FOR ONE MORE?

If there's room to stretch your budget, you might want to save yourself the hassle of coordinating one vehicle for so many people and rent additional limousines to transport attendants. But if your transportation budget is on the small side, some compromises are in order. Using one limousine necessitates an intricate series of passenger exchanges on the wedding day. Here's how it works: The bride gets the first ride in the limo, and it transports her, her parents, and the bridesmaids to the ceremony site. Time allowing, this limo could then return to pick up the groom and deliver him to the site as well. After the ceremony, the bride returns to the limousine with her groom, and the two of them ride to the reception.

Alternate scenario: You might have too many bridesmaids to fit all of them plus you and your parents in one trip. In this case, if your ceremony site is close enough to where you're getting ready, the limousine might be able make a first trip with just the bridesmaids, then come back for the rest of you. If this is not possible, ask your bridesmaids to ride to the ceremony on their own, and just go in the limo with your parents.

Large Luxury

After the ceremony, it's really important to shuffle everyone along to the place where you're taking pictures in an organized way. The photography process will flow more smoothly if everyone arrives at the site together, and you don't have to worry about any attendants getting lost on the way to the reception. Unless you have just a few bridesmaids and groomsmen, there's no way you'll fit all of them in one limo once the troops merge after the ceremony. Here again, you could rent multiple limos, but do the math first.

Budget Boosters: Transportation

◆ *Ask a friend or family member to borrow that vintage car or Lincoln Navigator—then ask your brother-in-law, cousin, or friend to do the driving.*

◆ *Hire a smaller limo or town car that will carry only you, the groom, and your parents, rather than a larger one to fit the entire wedding party.*

◆ *Opt for a small but social customized bus, an often cheaper (and fun) alternative to the traditional—and sometimes uncomfortable—limo.*

◆ *Enlist a smaller mom-and-pop limo shop. Often, these establishments will charge less than the dominant limousine fleet companies in your area, because they have less overhead and fewer advertising costs.*

◆ *Coordinate your ceremony and reception sites to be within walking distance, so that the entire wedding party, followed by guests, can hoof it to your reception.*

Classic Concerns: The Rental Length

Don't count on keeping your limo around until after your reception to drive you to your hotel or the airport until you look into those rates. Most limousine companies charge in four- or five-hour blocks of time, and then the rates increase hourly from there. That means you'll be paying for all those extra hours while your limo driver sits there parked at your reception.

There might be more economical options. These days, you can rent a super-sized SUV/limousine bus to carry you and your wedding party all around the town. These vehicles are luxury on wheels, and some can seat more than twenty people—yes, all at once. Pack everybody in, turn up the radio, pop the champagne, and get the party started right away.

These vehicles often end up functioning a lot like lounges, especially if there's a long break between your ceremony and reception. Park it at your picture taking site, fill it up with drinks and snacks, and send out the signal to your nearest and dearest who are there to watch. (Trust us—even your grandparents will be popping in and out for a break when they're not on call for pictures.)

LATE-NIGHT LOGISTICS

Okay, you have transportation for the ceremony and the reception covered, but does that leave you high and dry when it comes to getting to the hotel later on? Your bridesmaids and groomsmen are really on their own at this point. You might want to do a little advanced planning and drop their cars off at the reception site sometime before the wedding, or you could always ask a few friends and relatives to take over the chauffeuring duties after hours.

You and your groom will also have to make sure that you have a method for getting to your final destination. If you want to continue living in the lap of luxury, you could hire another car to drive you. You could also ride with family members or friends, or make arrangements to leave your own car in the parking lot at the reception. Just make sure to bring the keys along, too. You'll both be really bummed out if everyone else takes off without you.

Finding the Right Limo

Picture this. It's your wedding day. You're all dressed and ready to go; all you need now is the limousine. But it's late. Or it arrives on time, but it's covered in dirt and grime you just know is going to get all over your dress.

You probably won't just grin and bear these sorts of wedding-day nightmares, so do everything you can to prevent them ahead of time. A recently married friend or relative might be able to recommend a reliable limousine service with good cars—and thereby save you a lot of legwork. But if you're not that lucky, start checking around, and don't just ask questions over the phone. Get out there and look at the cars in person to be sure that you're getting all of the amenities you request.

DEAL WITH THE OWNER

Some limo services rent cars out from another company, which means several other services are probably sharing those cars as well. In addition to maintenance and overuse problems, it's harder for a company that doesn't own its own limos to ensure the availability of a specific car, or to supply you with a car of the color and size you want. That's why it's better to find a company that owns its limousines. Owners are more likely to keep track of a car's maintenance and whereabouts (you do not want to ride in a limo that has seen its share of unauthorized excursions).

Make sure you ask about a service's license and insurance coverage. Get references, then verify that the chauffeurs show up on time, are courteous, don't break the speed limit, and don't have a habit of crashing into trees.

Inspect all of the cars, and keep your eyes peeled for the following:

- Do they look modern and up-to-date or are they ready to fall apart?
- Are there obvious scratches or dents on the cars? (There shouldn't be.)
- Are the interior surfaces spotless when you get in to inspect the vehicles? (They should be.)
- Are the windows clean?
- Do the cars smell like smoke?
- Is there enough room for your groom and his linebacker buddies to spread out without crushing any crinolines?

Most importantly, make sure the company has the kind of limo you're looking for. Don't take a company's word that it can get you a black stretch limo with black leather interior. You shouldn't sign anything until you see it with your own eyes!

How Much?

Most limousine services charge by the hour. Unfortunately for you, the clock starts the second the driver leaves the base, not the moment he or she starts carting you around. Many companies offer package deals with a specific number of hours included in the price—but you need to understand what's included. A three-hour deal might sound like more than enough time (because you know you're not going to be sitting in that limo for three hours)—but if there's a delay between the ceremony and the reception (if you're getting married at one o'clock and your reception is at five, for example), you're going to need at least four-and-a-half hours.

Find out about exact costs. What, exactly, will you be getting for your money? Some limo companies can add extras like champagne, glasses, and ice, or balloons and flowers. Others also offer a "runner" service, which means that you can keep the driver "on call" to run home any guests who've imbibed a little too much bubbly at the reception.

Sign on the Dotted Line

Once you decide on a limousine service, get all the details finalized in a written contract. It should specify the type of car, additional options and services you will need, the expected length of service, the date, and the time. If there's a specific limo you just have to have (it's the only one with two sunroofs, or it's the only one with a DVD player), ask the owner to specify it on the contract. Ask about contingencies, too. If you're choosing the company's top-of-the-line car and something happens to it, where does that leave you? Get these details in writing.

The chauffeur's tip, usually 10 to 20 percent of the bill, is sometimes included in the fee, but read the fine print of your contract to find out for sure. You don't want to stiff someone who has helped to make your day run (or ride) smoothly. (Also speak up if you are dissatisfied with your chauffeur's service—don't be afraid to ask for your money back.)

Note: Be kind to your driver. He's a service provider, not your slave. And he certainly isn't being paid to be insulted or teased. If your attendants are giving the guy a hard time, step in. Otherwise, your chauffeur just might snap and leave you stranded out in the middle of nowhere!

Alternate Transportation

So you say limos aren't your thing? No problem; fortunately, options abound when it comes to wedding transportation.

HORSE AND CARRIAGE

This is *romance* on wheels. Before you choose this option, however, consider when your wedding will take place. If you're planning a winter wedding, at the very least you'll have to invest in a warm wrap. In areas that get hit hard by winter storms, it might be better to forgo this option. There's no way you're going to get a horse to pull that carriage down icy roads and through three feet of snow. Better to play it safe and hire something with a motor—and snow tires and a heater.

TROLLEYS

Trolleys offer the same kind of space as a limo bus, with the added allure of classic ambience. Many trolley rides are open-air affairs, but in colder climates, most offer some kind of protection from the elements.

ANTIQUE AUTOS

Renting luxury or antique cars is another good option if you're looking for something less conventional. Many limousine companies have a few classic cars on their lots; you can also look in your phone book under "Livery."

Presuming this option appeals to you and you have enough cash on hand, rent an antique model for you and your groom, then go with an additional limo or SUV for the wedding party. Just be sure you want to be separated from the rest of the crowd while you're joyriding. If you'd prefer to be whooping it up alongside family and friends, this might not be the best option for you.

Note: Renting an antique convertible might sound tempting if you're getting married in the warm weather. Before you go this route, however, consider whether you're okay with arriving at your wedding windswept. If you're paying to have your hair perfectly coiffed that morning, this may not be your best option.

Classic Rewind

Because transportation might not seem like a complicated decision, it's tempting to put it off. It's never too early to look into transportation. Don't forget that May and June are big prom and graduation months, and limos will be in high demand for these events as well. If you're unsure about how quickly transportation books up in your area, call some companies and ask for their recommendations.

Transportation Notes

Invitations

There are lots of supposed rules for wedding invitation protocol, and a lot depends on the style of your wedding. Beyond whether you choose elaborate or simple invitations, or whether the wording is formal or casual, there are other logistics to keep in mind. To begin with, you can't send out any invitations until you get your guest list squared away. Deciding who makes the cut can get messy, so consider your etiquette options carefully. You'll also want to compile a master list of all your guests' addresses *before* you're ready to send the invitations. There's nothing worse than scrambling around in a panic two days before you're scheduled to drop them in the mailbox.

Mastering the wedding invitation process also involves other details that might not readily come to mind, such as figuring out the required postage (this varies according to size and weight) and creating an organized system for stuffing all those envelopes. Follow the tips in this section, and you'll streamline and organize this typically tedious process.

Tally up Your Guests

Before you start looking through binder after binder of pretty wedding invitations, tackle the practicalities of the guest list. If you have a completely tension-free family life, an endless supply of wedding funds, unlimited reception space, and a magician who'll whip up a seating plan that pleases everyone, this is a cinch. But who are we kidding? In the real world, things rarely go so smoothly in this department.

Poised Under Pressure: **No Partial Invitations**

Never invite certain people to the ceremony but not the reception. That is like saying, "We like you enough to invite you to the free part, but not enough to pay for your dinner," and that's a major faux pas.

What happens when your parents think they're going to invite every last relative they can find, your coworkers assume they're all coming to your wedding, and you don't have enough room for everyone? Hit these problems head on; don't ignore them or push them aside until the last minute. These things have a way of blowing up in your face later on, once people get word of what's really going on.

YOUR VIP LIST

If you're on a budget, you'll have to do some fancy dancing when compiling your guest list. Start out by listing everyone you'd ideally like to invite. Split your list three ways: guests of the bride's parents, the groom's parents, and the couple. Look at how this first round shapes up—maybe you'll be pleasantly surprised to see the total number is within your reach.

If you do end up having to cut people, above all else, don't eliminate straight across the board at random. Some couples stick to a strictly mathematical approach and decide that each set of parents gets to invite one-third of the guests and then they get to invite the other third. This might not always be practical, however, if one side of the family is much larger than the other. In that case, a better approach is agreeing on certain boundary criteria and then sticking to them.

KIDS OR NO KIDS?

If you've decided not to invite children to your wedding, this fact is usually made clear to their parents by not including the children's names anywhere

Classic Concerns: **Don't Overlook the Obvious**

It's easy to get caught up in the details of the invitation process, but don't forget to include your parents, attendants, and officiant (and his or her spouse) in the final guest count. They should all receive formal invitations.

Classic Concerns: Set a Cutoff Point

If you don't invite children to your wedding, you'll need to pick a cutoff age to distinguish the gray area between "child" and "young adult." This is up to you and your fiancé, but eighteen or sixteen are common cutoff points. No matter what age you pick, make sure both families understand that they must adhere to that age—no exceptions.

on the invitation. Just to be safe, however, make sure your parents, your groom's parents, and anyone else who might be questioned is aware of your policy, so they can spread the word.

Whatever you decided in the end—it's essential that everyone play by the same rules. If there are children who are very special to you, consider making them part of the wedding; that way they'll be present for your big day, and you won't be offending anyone else.

COWORKERS AND DISTANT RELATIVES

One way to limit your guest list is by not inviting a slew of work acquaintances. This might be smart, especially if your office is very large and it's impractical to invite so many work people. Don't invite coworkers without their spouses. A better rule of thumb is to invite only those coworkers with whom you socialize outside of the immediate work environment, along with their significant others. Extending an invitation to an immediate superior can be a nice gesture if you are inviting other people from work, especially when office politics are of concern.

Likewise, you might not be able to invite distant relatives. Again, be consistent. As long as your third cousins don't have to hear that your second cousins twice removed have been invited, they should understand your need to cut costs.

Invite Etiquette

Once you get a handle on general guest-list issues, you can deal with the details. Should your guests be allowed to bring guests? Do you have to invite everyone who has invited you to their wedding in the past? If you receive a lot of regrets, can you fill those spaces with other people? There are plenty of delicate questions to navigate here; be careful.

GUEST PLUS ONE

When your guest list is tipping the scales, it's often tempting to invite people without a guest. Not so fast here. You should certainly allow people to bring their significant others. Married and engaged guests, guests who are living together, and those who are seriously dating should almost always be invited with their significant other. And, although not absolutely necessary, if possible, allow unattached guests to bring someone. This is especially important for those who might not know a lot of the people at your wedding, as it will help them feel more comfortable.

Always give your attendants the option to bring a date, even if they're not involved with anyone at the time. These people have worked hard (and taken on a hefty financial burden) to be part of your wedding. They deserve to share the day with someone special to them.

If you really can't afford to invite single guests with a date or if allowing single people to bring random guests will push you over the guest-list brink at your reception facility, don't be afraid to explain your position honestly to people. It's hard to stay mad at a bride who tries to be so diplomatic!

RETURNING THE FAVOR?

If a distant relative or acquaintance invited you to her wedding, this does not necessarily obligate you to invite her to yours. It's one thing if you're having a small affair and don't plan to invite your entire extended clan; however, you shouldn't just exclude people at random. Once again, the best approach is to be honest up front.

Poised Under Pressure: **Are They Relevant?**

If your parents (or stepparents) start to get out of control with their guest list, gently remind them that those guests should be relevant to you and your husband-to-be in some way. It's understandable if your parents want to invite a few old friends, but if they've got twenty-five extra people you hardly know tacked onto the list, it's only natural that you'd much prefer to fill those slots with some of your own friends.

Last-Minute Invites

Because it's realistic to anticipate some regrets (on average, about twenty to twenty-five percent of invited guests will be unable to attend), some couples decide to send a second mailing of invitations to another round of people once they see how many guests decline. Unless you want to come off as really tacky and uncouth, avoid this tactic at all costs!

Fact Checking

Once you've finalized your guest list, start typing it up on your computer. Be sure you have all of the correct information. Double check the spelling of names, verify the proper titles (doctors, clergy members, military personnel, and so on), and track down the right addresses. You might also want to list phone numbers; they'll come in handy if you need to call someone who's late with an R.S.V.P., or if any family members or friends want to contact guests to invite them to showers or other parties. You're killing two birds with one stone here, because once your wedding is over, you'll be glad you have a master database of all the important people in your life.

The Invitation Search

After you finish all the prep work, you're ready to choose the actual invitations. The look of your invitation gives people their first inkling about what type of wedding you'll be having. If you send out invitations with a colorful bunch of balloons on the front that proclaim "We're Having a Party!" they probably won't be expecting a formal affair with top hats and tails. Conversely, an elegantly engraved invitation is bound to give people the message not to show up in jeans. Choose appropriate invitations.

THE OLD-FASHIONED METHOD

Most brides still find their invitations by going to a stationery supplier and browsing through catalogs. These catalogs contain samples of predesigned invitations so you can see options for paper color, paper stock, borders, and ornamentation. Many invitations come complete with phrasing options; your stationer will be able to help you decide on this.

Because a handful of companies supply the vast majority of wedding invitations, you'll probably come across the same sample catalogs in most of the places you look. That means there's no need to waste time comparing one stationer to another. As long as you find someone with whom you're comfortable, and that stationer offers you a good price, you should be all set.

INTERNET INVITES

There are countless Web sites that sell traditional as well as unusual invitations, and if you're looking for a real deal, you'll find it here. The downside,

---

Classic Concerns: Endless Options

When you look for your invitations, be prepared to flip through samples until your eyes glaze over; there are that many choices. If you normally have a hard time choosing between many options, take someone along who will help you narrow down the choices. Your mom or your maid of honor can act as the voice of reason if you find yourself overwhelmed by all the options.

Poised Under Pressure: Host a Girls' Invitation Night

Addressing the invitations is a tedious, exacting task. Don't wait around for the men to volunteer to pitch in here—they usually just don't understand why you have to include the tissue paper or stack the invitation, response card, and directions a certain way. Enlist your mom, grandma, girlfriends, or any other women you know who might be up for the challenge, and make a girls' night of it!

of course, is that you're taking a chance. Many brides like to see and feel their prospective invitations. If you receive a box of two hundred invitations with fuzzy printing on flimsy paper, the money you save will be worth nothing and you'll instantly regret your choice. Before you go the Internet route, educate yourself about things like paper stock, acid-free paper, and various printing methods. Order samples first, so you can see the quality of the company's printing.

If you don't have the time (or the interest) for a crash course on the finer points of paper and ink, you're better off ordering invitations from a store. This way, you can ask questions and actually see what you're ordering.

SPECIALTY PRINTERS

If you can't find an invitation you like online or in a stationery store, private printers can do the job for you. These printers might be a bit harder to find and more expensive than the big guys, but if you want your invitations to feature goats playing football instead of the typical flowers, doves, or bells (they're *your* invitations), this might be your best bet. Check the business section of your phone directory under "Printers." Just be sure it's worth it to exert the extra time and expense this will take.

Printing Techniques

When it comes to ordering your wedding invitations, the type of print you choose is a big factor in how much (or how little) you spend. Here's a brief rundown of your options:

♦ **Engraving:** This elegant option involves "stamping" the paper from the back. Using metal plates a printer creates, the technique raises the letters up off of the paper as they're printed. Unfortunately, you'll pay extra for all that elegance, so unless you're prepared to spend a pretty penny, this might be out of your league.

♦ **Thermography:** This is a great way to get the look of engraving at about half the price. By using a special press that heats the ink, the

Budget Boosters: Invitations

♦ *If you really want custom-made invitations, but you're afraid you can't afford them, hire a graphic arts student to design your dream invitation. They won't charge as much as a freelance artist or design studio.*

♦ *Skip the engraving for significant savings; invitations look and feel just as elegant with today's less-expensive raised printing methods.*

♦ *Nix the calligrapher and address invites yourself. You might get caught up in the idea of calligraphy because it seems fancy or high-class, but be realistic. No one else will really care that much, and guests are just going to throw out the invitation envelopes anyway.*

♦ *Remember to factor in postage costs when choosing your invitations. Unusually shaped or oversized invitations require additional postage, and those costs can really add up. Talk to your stationer about minimizing the final weight of the invitation.*

♦ *Consider designing your R.S.V.P. card as a postcard to save postage costs as well. Postcards are an efficient and convenient way of tracking responses—and no tiny envelopes to open!*

printer creates a raised-letter effect that is almost indistinguishable from engraving. (Most mass-produced invitations are done using this method.)

◆ **Offset printing:** Also called lithography, this technique produces flat images and is the starting point for thermography.

◆ **Calligraphy:** Printers are now able to reproduce calligraphy using software—a method considerably faster (and cheaper) than the human hand.

Choice of Wording

Having trouble figuring out how to word your invitations? You're not alone. With all the mixed families in the world today, many couples find themselves in a quandary wondering how not to offend anyone. Relax—there are as many options for wording styles as there are invitation designs. First think about who is hosting the wedding and whose names you would like to include on the invitation, then your stationer will help you to figure the rest out. There are a number of possibilities that have bearing when it comes to the wording on your invitations:

◆ Are either the bride or groom's parents hosting the wedding, or are both sets of parents hosting jointly?

◆ Is either set of parents divorced? (Circumstances vary when divorced parents host a wedding, depending on whether the parents are remarried or not, and whether the bride or groom wishes to list their stepparents as well.)

◆ Are any of your parents deceased? If so, has your other parent remarried? (Deceased parents are usually not mentioned on wedding invitations because only the hosts of the event are listed. However, if you want to adapt your invitation wording to mention your late mother or father, you certainly can.)

◆ Will some other close friend or relative act as wedding host? (If, for example, your grandparents raised you, this might be the case.)

- Are you and the groom hosting the wedding yourselves?

- Would you like to emphasize the religious aspect of your marriage? Consult your officiant prior to having the invitations printed, because wordings change according to denominations.

- Are any of the people who will be listed on your invitations involved in the military? In military weddings, rank determines the placement of names.

Invitation Extras

As if choosing the invitations and wording them carefully isn't enough— you'll still have choices to make about the envelopes, you'll also need to inform your guests about the particulars of the ceremony and reception, as well as provide them with directions and other details.

ENVELOPES

Like the invitations themselves, the envelopes you choose can range from simple, with plain, high-quality paper, to fancy, with foil-laminated inner flaps or flaps with a colorful design. Beautifully packaged invitations are a nice touch, although (not surprisingly) the more you add to the envelope the greater the cost.

Plan to have the return address preprinted on the invitation's outer envelopes and response cards. Traditionally, whoever is listed as the host for the wedding receives the R.S.V.P.s. If *you're* the one communicating with the reception site coordinator or caterer (even though your parents are the actual hosts) you might prefer to have the responses sent directly to you. If, however, your parents volunteer to take on the task of receiving responses, don't argue. Keeping track of all the R.S.V.P.s is a time-consuming task; you'll be happy they offered to help you out in this area when the going gets really tough toward the end of your planning!

Classic Concerns: Address Labels

Etiquette snobs will tell you that you can't preprint your invitation addresses. If you have the time and inclination to handwrite them yourself—or the budget to hire a calligrapher—more power to you. If, however, it will help you to save time and reduce your stress level, preprint away! Most computers today provide a range of colors and fonts. Choose one that matches your invitation style and type up labels or print addresses directly onto envelopes.

RECEPTION AND RESPONSE CARDS

If the reception is at a different location than the ceremony, you'll need to include reception cards in your invitations. Remember to include the full address of the reception site for out-of-town guests. You'll also need to include response cards; these are the cards that guests send back to you so that you can add them to your final list or scratch them from it. If dinner will be served, make that clear, and provide the dinner choices.

Don't forget that the response cards also need an envelope, complete with first-class postage stamp.

When to Order

Order your invitations three to four months before the wedding, and always order more than you need, because you will make mistakes while you're addressing envelopes. If you have at least twenty extra invitations on hand, it will lessen the tensions among those writing them out and will save you the money of having to place a second order. (The majority of charges for your invitation are for the initial startup of the press; adding a few more to your initial order is much cheaper than placing reorders.)

Your goal is to get your invitations out in the mail six to eight weeks before the wedding, so plan your prep time accordingly. (If you're planning a wedding near a holiday, mail out your invitations a few weeks earlier to give your guests some extra time to plan.) Set an R.S.V.P. date of two or three weeks before the wedding; this will give you a comfortable cushion as you work out your seating arrangements and confirm dinner choices with your caterer or reception facility.

Addressing Invitations

This is a massive undertaking. You'd think it would be fun and exciting— you're sending out wedding invitations for the biggest day of your life, after all! But actually, it's more an exercise in exacting tedium. Give yourself plenty of time to accomplish this task, and be realistic: Don't think you're going to write out several hundred envelopes in one sitting.

Hospitality for the Out-of-Towners

Go the extra mile if you've got out-of-town guests. Check to see if you can get lower rates for reserving a block of hotel rooms. Be sure to detail the prices and special features of the accommodations you've reserved and include this with your invitations.

For the benefit of guests who will be flying out, include the names and numbers of some rental car agencies with your invitations. If they'll be relying on public transportation, send them a map of the subway, train, or bus system in your city. Don't forget to enclose detailed maps and directions to all the events for those unfamiliar with the area.

If out-of-town guests must bring children who are not invited to the wedding with them for the trip, arrange for a babysitter well in advance. (Many hotels also provide this service for weddings.)

Also be sure to include things to do while your guests have free time: Suggest movie theaters, restaurants, bars, parks, and any regional events such as fairs or outdoor concerts that will take place while they're in town.

Poised Under Pressure: **Stay on Top of Stragglers**

When it comes to sending out wedding invitations, it's always best to assume that some stragglers will respond late. Set a response date far enough in advance of your wedding so that you can make the appropriate phone calls to those oblivious souls who neglect to return your card and ask whether they will be attending or not.

Ask a few people to help you address your invitations, but don't ask so many that things become chaotic. Make sure the same person who writes the information on the inside of an invitation also addresses its outer envelope.

Packing Them Up

Yes, there is a specific method to all of this madness. What goes where, and why? Here's a system that should make things easier for you:

1. Place the response card face up under the flap of the response card envelope.

2. Place a small piece of tissue paper over the lettering on the invitation.

3. Put any extra enclosures (reception cards, maps, directions, etc.) inside the invitation. Put the response card and envelope inside the invitation as well. The lettering should be facing upward.

4. Place the invitation inside the inner envelope with the lettering facing the back flap. Don't seal this envelope. (The inner envelope is not typically gummed anyway.)

5. Put the inner envelope inside the outer envelope; again, the writing on the inner envelope should face the flap of the outer envelope.

6. Seal the outer envelope. Make sure the envelope is properly addressed and contains your return address.

7. Stamp and mail.

Postage Peace of Mind

Imagine the horror of sending out all of your invitations, only to have them returned to you for improper postage. Just to be on the safe side, take one sample that's completely packaged and ready to go to the post office and have it weighed before you send out the entire batch. An invitation that's an odd shape (square instead of rectangle, for instance) might also require extra postage and a little extra time.

Classic Rewind

People sometimes behave in strange ways or do things they normally wouldn't when large sums of money are involved. This could not be more true in the case of a wedding. Yes, this is your day and you're entitled to invite (or not invite) whomever you like, but use a little common sense—and common decency. Take people's feelings and comfort level into account wherever possible, and do your best to be accommodating. (After all, would you like to go to somebody's wedding with no date when you know hardly any of the other guests?)

Invitations should only be ordered after you've verified the details of your ceremony and reception. Double-check times and confirm the location addresses. (You wouldn't want to print invitations with an incorrect street number!) Order invitations two to three months before the wedding, but not before your guest list is finalized, so that you're sure you have enough.

Invitation Notes

Additional Pertinent Details

So you're set with your photographer and videographer, you've chosen a band or DJ, the transportation is in place, and the dresses and tuxes have been ordered. You still have a few more hoops to jump through before you actually tie the knot. You need to pick out your rings, for starters. And, of course, there are those little legalities, like the marriage license and a blood test, in the case of some states—don't forget to plan ahead for these essentials! This section will also help you to navigate other details, such as creating great favors and ceremony programs, changing your name—or not—and so on.

Ring Quest

When you and your fiancé are ready to shop for your wedding rings, your first step should be consulting with a reputable jeweler. Pick a store that appeals to you, stocks jewelry in your price range, and is a member of the American Gem Society. Nevertheless, avoid taking any chances, and keep the following tips in mind:

1. **Shop around.** Even if you fall head over heels in love with the first ring you set eyes on, a little perspective never hurt anyone. Comparing selections from other jewelers will give you a wider variety of options and help you to determine fair prices. Beware of shops that pressure you to buy on the spot.

2. **Negotiate.** Don't hesitate to ask if the price is negotiable. Most jewelry salespeople expect to do their fair share of haggling.

3. **Before the sale is final, take the ring to an appraiser of your choice to verify value and price.** There's nothing rude about requesting to do this; reputable jewelers will understand your concern. This way, you'll be sure you're not dealing with a jeweler who might try to dupe you into buying a ring for more than it's worth by having their own appraiser "confirm" the ring's inflated value.

4. **Make sure your purchase agreement includes stipulations for sizing and potential return.** Does the store offer a money-back guarantee if the ring is returned within the designated time frame? Also, any resizing, tightening, or cleaning required during the first six months of ownership should be free.

5. **After you do purchase your rings, get a written appraisal and insurance.** Losing your wedding ring is probably the last thing on your mind as you anticipate your wedding day, but don't put this on the back burner. Insurance requires that you get a written appraisal describing your rings and stating their value. Insure your rings under your homeowner's or renter's policy. You'll rest easier knowing you're covered, just in case.

The Marriage License

The ins and outs of obtaining a marriage license vary from state to state. Contact your local marriage bureau (usually in the city clerk's office) to find out what steps you have to take and how much time is involved. Generally, you should start the actual license process one month before your wedding, but if you need to get hold of your birth certificates and other records from out of state, start tracking those things down well in advance.

Also be aware that in most cases, the window of opportunity with marriage licenses is narrow and strict. You can't apply for your marriage license too early, as marriage licenses do expire. They're usually good for between thirty and ninety days, but this varies from state to state. In some areas, the license might be good for just thirty days, while in others, it lasts six months or more. Additionally, some states require a waiting period, usually between three and five days, from application to receipt of the marriage license. Check with the state in which you're getting married for specifics. (Remember, the marriage license must be obtained from the state in which you're getting married, not the state where you reside.)

DRAWING BLOOD

In certain states (plus the District of Columbia), you might also need to take a blood test before you can obtain your marriage license. Some states still require testing for syphilis, and a few test for rubella as well. (Also known as German measles, this disease is dangerous to unborn babies.) Check with your specific state to be absolutely sure of what you need to do.

Due to the rise in HIV and AIDS, many states now also require that individuals applying for a marriage license must receive information on available HIV/AIDS testing. Although no states presently require a mandatory premarital HIV/AIDS test, many doctors strongly suggest it.

The Rules of Engagement (and Marriage)

Regardless of where you get married, you will need to follow some basic guidelines common to all states:

- You and your groom must apply for the license together.
- You must both have all of the required paperwork ready, including birth certificate, driver's license, proof of age, and proof of citizenship.
- In the case of previous marriage, you must provide proof of divorce or annulment.
- You need to pay a fee. This fee ranges from $10 or $20 in some states to as much as $80 in others.
- Be prepared to state your intention. The people at the city clerk's office will ask you to verify that you weren't coerced into marriage.
- When you sign the license, you should already have decided on what your married name will be. The license is the first legal document you will sign with your new (or old) name, so make sure you write it exactly as you want it to be.

Be aware that many states will only accept cash as payment.

DOES A MARRIAGE LICENSE MEAN YOU'RE MARRIED?

Having a marriage license doesn't mean you are legally married; it just means you have the state's permission to get married. In order to be valid and truly binding, the license has to be signed by a religious or civil official. Someone must give your officiant the license before the ceremony starts. Then the officiant simply signs the license once the ceremony is complete and sends it back to the proper state office.

Wait until you've received a copy of your marriage license before you change your name on any documents. In many instances (when changing your name on bank accounts, for example), you'll need proof that you are who you say you are, and your marriage license is confirmation of that.

Changing Your Name—or Not

In years past, it was commonly accepted that women simply relinquished any claim to their birth name and automatically took their husband's name once married. Today, however, there's more room for individual choice. Even if you've always taken your own last name for granted, you might be surprised at how much it means to you once you're faced with its possible loss. After all, this is your family's name—the name you identify with and the name by which everyone else identifies you. It's bound to be tough letting it go. On the other hand, if your last name is ten syllables long, and no one can ever even pronounce it right, you might be ready for a change.

If taking your husband's name is an easy decision for you, congratulations. Your life will be much simpler if you're not filled with inner conflict over this issue. For many brides, however, this decision is quite difficult. Women now choose all sorts of options to accommodate just about any name combination or situation. If you are in a quandary over names, remember that ultimately, the only opinions that matter are yours and your husband's.

That said, be ready for some confusion if you do decide to keep your maiden name. Although it's becoming increasingly common, if you decide to do so, you'll soon learn that everyone from your Great Aunt Rita to the lady at the bridal shop will think nothing of assuming that you're taking your husband's name. You're in for plenty of questions and quizzical expressions as you explain—time and time again, in some cases. And even if you take great pains to make your name choice clear on your wedding program, announcements, thank-you notes, and all other subsequent methods of communication, you'll still have to get used to the idea of lots of people sending you things addressed to Mrs. John Smith. Don't go crazy on people; be patient, keep reminding everyone politely, and don't worry about what anyone else thinks.

Also, don't read the riot act to someone who innocently addresses you as a Mrs. because you've just met them or they don't know your circumstances. If, however, your sister-in-law introduces you by the wrong name for the twentieth time, you should say something. Better yet, avoid this awkwardness by taking initiative and introducing yourself to strangers first, where it's appropriate: "Hi, I'm Jennifer Andrews, Richard Miller's wife."

START SPREADING THE NEWS

You can inform people of your decision on the name question in one grand swoop, or through a series of individual notices. A newspaper announcement will reach the most people the fastest. If you're aiming for a more personal touch, you can always send out cards that include your name choice. As for the wording, try something like: "The bride will keep her name." Or, if you really want to drive the message home, be direct: "Jennifer Andrews and Richard Miller wish to announce that both will keep their present names for all legal and social purposes" or "Jennifer Andrews announces that she will take the surname Miller after her marriage on June 5, 2005."

If you do decide to take your husband's last name, you've also got your work cut out for you, but it's not *so bad*. Fortunately, changing your name when you get married is a lot easier than changing it just for kicks. Signing your name on the marriage license is proof of your new name; now you just have to inform the appropriate people. Here's a list to help you keep track of all the places you'll need to notify regarding your new marital status and your change of name and/or address.

401(k) accounts

Automotive insurance

Bank accounts

Billing accounts

Car registration

Club memberships

Credit cards

Dentist

Doctors

Driver's license

Employment records

Homeowner's/renter's insurance

IRA accounts

Leases

Life insurance

Loans

Medical insurance

Other insurance accounts

Passport

Pension plan records

Post office

Property titles

Safety deposit box

School records

Social Security

Stocks and bonds

Subscriptions

Telephone listing

Utilities

Voter registration records

Wills/trusts

Other (list separately)

Note: Your husband can use a similar list to notify the appropriate people about his new address, change in marital status, and so on.

Wedding Favors

In life, it's the little things that count, and weddings are no exception. The small touches you add to your wedding will give the day a personalized stamp and show your guests how happy you are to have them there to celebrate with you. Your budget will dictate how much you can spend, but keep in mind that a little creativity in this department can go a long way toward cutting costs.

If you're creative, and have the time, great! In that case, go ahead and make something special. But if you don't have the time or you're all thumbs when it comes to crafts, that's okay, too. You'll find plenty of ideas for favors that come ready-made.

Whatever you decide about your favors, one thing's for sure. The days of giving useless little trinkets are long gone. Increasingly, couples are opting for meaningful favors that serve a purpose or reflect their personalities. If you're the crafty type, there are plenty of unique favors you can make yourself. Invite a few friends over, and have a favor-making party.

Note: If you choose to have favors that you'll want to engrave, remember to allow enough time so you don't have to run around picking them up just before the wedding.

ALL THE POSSIBILITIES

Following are some creative ideas for favors. (Wherever possible, check to see if you can get a discount for buying in bulk.)

◆ **Frames** that hold the names of each guest can be used as place cards at the reception and also serve as favors. Shop around at craft supply stores, party stores, or on the Internet.

◆ **Candles** also make a lovely gift and you can go inexpensive or expensive as you wish. You can also decorate them: Wrap each with tulle and ribbons, and add extra details like tiny seashells if you'd like.

◆ **Decorative soaps** are inexpensive and easy to make. You can find molds and materials in most craft stores. Or simply buy some inexpensive, colorful soaps, then wrap and decorate yourself.

◆ **Inexpensive wine glasses** also make great gifts. Use a gold or silver craft pen to inscribe your names and the date of the wedding on each one, or use faux engraving kits. Add a creative design, or a engrave a line from your favorite poem, and you'll turn a simple, everyday item into something special.

◆ **Candy:** There are companies that make candy bar or lollipop wrappers printed with your own special message. If you're really creative, and you have a scanner, make the wrappers yourself. Guests will get a big kick out of a chocolate bar wrapped in your favorite snapshots.

- **Flower seeds or tree seedlings:** If you and your groom love nature, this is a good option. Make a card to go along with your gift telling guests how to plant them. Then, your guests will think fondly of your wedding day whenever they look at these plants in the years to come. Some companies will print your names on seed packets.

- **Wine:** Some companies offer tiny, individual-sized bottles that sit nicely on tables at your reception. Others personalize full-size bottles. These are great to leave at your hotel's reception desk, to welcome out-of-town guests when they check in.

- **Donations:** Many couples are opting to eschew individual gifts for each guest, deciding instead to make a donation to a favorite charity. Whether you and your husband-to-be are animal lovers or have an attachment to a particular medical research fund, there are many ways to get creative with this meaningful gift. Consider making your own decorated scrolls explaining your charity of choice, or place one larger, fancy frame at each table highlighting your cause. If you go for the frames, you can always give them away as mementos at the end to special people at your reception.

Most local party stores and Internet wedding-supply sites offer fun boxes for favors in just about any shape, size, and price you can imagine. These little boxes add a fresh touch to simple favors such as a handful of Hershey's kisses or Jordan almonds. Grab some cute tags from your nearest office supply or stationery store, and you've got a unique gift.

The Wedding Program

A printed program of your ceremony is a wonderful way for your guests to follow along. You can have the same person who is doing your wedding invitations prepare your programs, or you can create them yourself. Programs are easy to print on your own computer—and that makes them relatively inexpensive, too. Many office supply and stationery stores have program covers and paper varieties to choose from. The rest is up to you.

Sure, your wedding program is the proper place to outline everything that will happen during your ceremony, but it's also a great way to communicate with your guests about other things. In addition to listing your ceremony readings and songs, you can give credit to your bridesmaids and groomsmen, thank your guests for attending, and express your gratitude to your families for helping you through the wedding process. Try some of these techniques:

◆ Instead of simply listing the names of your wedding party, include a short, pithy, or funny description of each individual.

◆ Scan some photos or other images you and your fiancé choose yourselves to make your program more personal.

◆ Share some pertinent details about your relationship. While no one wants to read a novel-length wedding program, short snippets about how you and your groom met will add extra meaning.

◆ Include a few lines from a favorite song, poem, Bible passage, or some other quote that reflects the meaning of your special day.

◆ Explain the meaning of various ceremony practices especially if you are having an interfaith wedding or including unfamiliar rituals or traditions.

Your reception will be hectic, and it's not always easy to speak to every guest individually. Your wedding program is a great opportunity to communicate personal feelings about your wedding day, your guests, and each other.

Classic Rewind

Things should be coming together for you by this point. But don't stop there. It's absolutely imperative that you stay on top of the legalities (you won't have a wedding without arranging for your marriage license in time). But not everything at this stage of the game is a legal drag. Set aside time to plan programs, favors, and other creative wedding tasks. If you're realistic in your timeframes and goals, you'll look forward to accomplishing these details, and they'll serve as a nice break from all of the budget planning and vendor consultations that have been occupying so much of your time.

Before and After

take a break

You've reached a point where you can forgo stress and enjoy luxury, relaxation, and wonderful cuisine! Your bridal shower and other festivities are the time to sit back and enjoy quality time with those you love.

The Bridal Shower

At last, something that you're not responsible for planning! Or sort of, at least. Sure, your mom, grandmas, sisters, aunts, cousins, bridesmaids, and other friends will probably all want to get in on the shower-planning action, but that doesn't necessarily mean they won't need your input on where and when to have the shower, who to invite, what to eat, and so on. Enjoy your shower: In the midst of wedding-planning anxiety, this day stands out as a tiny oasis of serenity and relaxation. It's a time for you to pause, catch your breath, kick back, and enjoy some good times with the people you love.

Shower Specifics

Chances are, lots of people in your life are very excited about your impending marriage, and they're all going to want to plan wonderful events in your honor, so be for plenty of socializing. If someone offers to throw a shower for you, don't look a gift horse in the mouth. This is no time to be modest or avoid the spotlight. You should only decline in the most bizarre circumstances (say, for instance, your former boyfriend's new girlfriend wants to throw a party for you, and you two *are not* pals).

Showers are typically held at a restaurant, a small function hall, or in someone's home, depending on the size of the guest list. The guests are usually women, but your fiancé can come along for the ride if he wants. For that matter, if you're extremely close to your brother, male cousins, or guy friends and they want to be there, too, there's no reason why your shower couldn't be co-ed.

WHO'S THROWING YOUR SHOWER?

In the past, etiquette dictated that friends and not family members should host a bridal shower. Today, however, that's changed. Family, friends, coworkers, and anyone else who is so inclined can throw a shower for you. The most common hosts are your bridal party, in combination with your mother and other close family members—but who's to say which other generous (and ambitious) people might have a party up their sleeves?

Classic Concerns: **Choose Your Games Wisely!**

Many people like to keep things lively at showers by playing a few games. A word to the wise: Keep it clean. It's one thing to play rowdy games when you're sitting around with your girlfriends—it's quite another to include Grandma and Great Aunt Ruth. Too many racy antics will send them packing, so save it for your bachelorette party!

Poised Under Pressure: **Shower Juggling**

If you can, make all of your hosts aware of other showers being planned, so that they don't accidentally overlap. Knowing you're having more than one shower, they might want to gear each party in a different direction. Your friends could host a lingerie shower; your coworkers could throw a pantry-stocking party, and your family might plan a domestic/housewares party.

WHEN TO HAVE THE SHOWER

It used to be that the specifics of the shower—time, date, location, and so on—were kept secret from the bride until the last possible moment. These days, however, it's common—and in many cases, necessary—for the bride to take an active part in planning the festivities. Modern brides are usually far too busy to leave these things to chance.

Showers are usually held two to three months before the wedding date. If you absolutely cannot corral your most important guests within the confines of this time frame, shoot for a slightly earlier date or one that's a *little* closer to the wedding. Just make sure it's no more than a month before the big day—you'll be insanely busy by that point.

INVITING THE GUESTS

Since you're the one who knows best who you want at your shower, you'll probably have to supply your shower hosts with a guest list. Touch base on the budget first. If your hosts are renting out a huge banquet hall, accommodating fifty guests shouldn't be a problem, but it will matter if they're planning a small, informal affair at someone's tiny apartment. In either case, who should be invited, and who should be left off the list?

THE CARDINAL RULE

Any guest who is invited to the shower is automatically invited to the wedding. Period. You can't get around this one, and if you try to, you'll look like a greedy and insensitive Bridezilla. Even if you know *you're* sticking to this rule, it's in your best interest to make sure your *hosts* aren't inviting women who aren't on your wedding guest list. If someone does slip through the cracks, you're going to be forced to add another place setting at your reception—which isn't the worst thing in the world. When you have to add *twenty* extra place settings, however, things will get hairy.

Shower Style

Different groups of people in your life might want to host separate showers for you. Your friends might want to throw you a girls'-night bachelorette party on the town, your coworkers might want to have another party; your mother will probably plan a family event, and then your groom's mother could set up something for their side. When it comes to showers, the more the merrier. Revel in all that attention!

SHOWER SIZE

Informal showers are generally a breeze to plan. Your hosts might want to send invitations but it's perfectly acceptable for the hosts to make phone calls if your guest list is small enough.

If you're a bride with a large family and many close friends, you'll probably find yourself in the midst of a huge shower. Some brides feel overwhelmed by the attention and the sheer volume of gifts. Here are some tips for navigating the large shower:

Poised Under Pressure: **Take a Break**

Set your stress aside, and enjoy the fun of your shower. It will feel great when someone else scouts the location, plans the food, and invites the guests. There's no need for overinvolvement here: Your biggest concern at this point is morning brunch or afternoon lunch, omelets or hors d'oeuvres.

- **Stay cool:** Even if you're completely overwhelmed, every guest wants to see you looking happy.

- **Mingle:** All of these women have come to celebrate your impending marriage, and they brought you gifts. Say hello to every single one of them.

- **Feed yourself:** You'll need nourishment if you want to keep pace opening all those presents. If you know you get really cranky when feeling crowded or hungry, don't turn a potentially bad situation into a disaster!

- **Fudge it:** Every gift deserves a sincere "ooh" and "ahh," even if you're losing steam when you're only halfway through the pile. Chances are you won't have to fudge it, though, once you see how much fun this can be!

THE IN-LAW SHOWER

If your future in-laws host a shower for you, you might be meeting many of your husband's extended relatives for the first time. Don't feel awkward. Remember, no one is forcing these women to come to your shower. They're there because they *want* to meet you and bring you gifts. Chances are (unless your husband-to-be has a really horrible family—in which case, they probably wouldn't be throwing you a shower to begin with) these people are really nice, and they want to like you. As corny as it might sound, all you need to do is be yourself, smile and say thank you, and make as much polite conversation as you can.

Classic Rewind

There's nothing worse than a bride who seems on edge during prewedding parties. Sure, all of the hoopla can seem overwhelming at times, but you shouldn't come across as "difficult," "bratty," or "spoiled rotten." Don't act as though someone forced you to come to your own shower and then waltz out with all the goodies. Most likely, lots of people will work hard to plan a special day for you. Be a gracious, grateful bride, you lucky girl!

Bridal Shower Notes

The Gift Registry

As an addendum to the shower, the other good news is your bridal registry. This is one of the (supposedly) more enjoyable aspects of the wedding planning process. After all, what could be better than complete license to run through a store zapping any and every item that strikes your fancy? Be prepared, however. You need to start registering far enough in advance to give yourself time, but not too far in advance. Pace yourself by spreading the registering process out over the course of a few trips, and brace yourself for setbacks. Store computers break, cashiers forget to take things off of your registry, items you selected months ago are suddenly no longer available . . . it's not as easy as it looks!

Gift registry is a free service provided by many department, jewelry, gift, and specialty stores. You and your groom simply pick out the gifts you'd like to receive, scan them into a computer registry, and then when friends and family go into the stores, they can pull up your registry on a touch-screen computer that stores the information. Many registries are also available online, through a store's Web site. As each item is bought, it is (theoretically) removed from the list, helping to prevent duplication.

Gift Etiquette

Before we get to the fun part of actually registering, a word of advice: Never include your registry information with your wedding invitation. It's fine,

Classic Concerns: **Why Registering Makes Sense**

Some couples are afraid to register because they think this makes them appear gift-greedy. This is not at all the case. Registries simply help to point your guests in the right direction. People are going to buy you gifts one way or another, and what good is it if you get Art Deco when you really wanted French Country? Remember, the alternative to registering is staring at a heap of gifts that contains five juicers, three blenders, and twelve can openers.

however, to list where you're registered on a bridal shower invitation. Most stores will provide you with little registry cards to include with shower invitations, or you can easily make them yourself.

Never request cash on any invitation, even if you need cash more than you need the gifts. Instead, ask your parents or other family members to pass the word along discreetly.

On the other hand, if you really feel you have everything you need, you can certainly request that guests don't bring gifts. Just don't print the request right on an invitation.

Choosing the Stores

You and your fiancé should think carefully about where you register. Make sure each store has a variety of quality items in the colors and styles you want. You might want to register at a particular specialty shop, but remember this does you no good if the store has no locations where many of your guests live and they don't have a Web site for guests to purchase online. In this instance, you probably won't get many of the gifts you chose.

Go ahead and register for a few special items in a small boutique if you'd like, but reserve the lion's share of your registry for a store that is easily accessible to the majority of your guests. It's best to register with at least one high-quality department store that is sure to have almost everything you need.

Poised Under Pressure: Stay on Top of Your Registry

No matter what the stores you register at tell you, chances are, mistakes are going to be made when it comes to removing gifts from your list once they've been bought. If you're saddled with four of the same slow cooker at your shower, something's definitely run amok. Be assertive with your registry store and explain that you need to be sure items are removed properly.

Classic Concerns: **The Proper Time Frame**

Most stores will tell you that you shouldn't register more than five or six months before your wedding, because items change and get discontinued a few times a year. Even if you do wait, however, some things will still be discontinued by the time your shower or wedding rolls around; items change that frequently. You might have to register at several different stores to find all of the items you're looking for, but that's okay.

Your registry will be sent to their branches in other cities and states and will also appear on their Web site—key advantages for out-of-town guests.

Before registering with a store, ask about the policy on returns and exchanges—you don't want to get stuck with duplicate or damaged gifts. Also make sure the store will take responsibility if you receive gifts intended for another couple, and vice versa. Inquire about any discounts you'll receive after your wedding as well. Many stores offer brides and grooms a certain percentage off of the merchandise that remains on their registry, so they can fill in what's missing.

GETTING STARTED

Don't rush the registering process. You'll have a lot to accomplish, and it gets overwhelming. Take your time, browse through the store, and register in stages, over the course of several different days, if need be. You don't want to choose important items like your formal (china) and everyday dinnerware patterns, silverware pattern, wine glasses, pots and pans, linens, bedding ensemble, or small appliances, while you're on sensory overload!

Many couples know exactly what they're looking for before they step foot in the store; others don't have the foggiest notion. Fortunately, most stores have preprinted registry sheets that will not only alert you to what you should be looking for, they'll practically walk you through the entire registering process. Once you decide on the styles, patterns, and colors you want, all you have to do is add the items to your list and fill in the quantity.

Poised Under Pressure: **Pricey Items**

Even though you might feel awkward about it, don't be afraid to ask for a few "big ticket" items like a television, VCR, or microwave. Most likely, some of your friends or family members will be looking to chip in together to buy you just such a gift.

Keeping Tabs on Gifts

At your shower, put someone you trust (an organized bridesmaid, your mother, a friend—but not your six-year-old niece) in charge of recording each gift and who gave it. Choose someone who can keep things organized even if things get hectic, so that when you sit down to write your thank-you notes, you won't come off sounding like a confused bride.

Be sure the person charged with keeping track of who gave you which gift understands the importance of the task. You *don't* want to see this person chit-chatting on her cell phone or hitting the buffet while you're working your way through the stack of presents.

Returning or Exchanging Gifts

What if someone sends you a lava lamp—with a matching fringe lampshade? Assuming your decorating instincts run in a different direction, you might be inclined to exchange it as fast as you can. But it's not that simple.

The best thing you can do to avoid this awkward situation is to wait until about a month after the wedding to exchange any unwanted gifts. Some brides display all of the gifts they've received somewhere in their home in the days before the wedding; anyone visiting at that time is likely to look for their gift and even ask your opinion of it.

After the wedding, when everything is put away in its proper place, guests are (hopefully) less likely to make an issue of their gifts.

Classic Concerns: Check I.D.

The last thing you want when you register is to receive the wrong gifts because they're intended for another bride with the same surname as you. Make sure the store uses your groom's name and/or your wedding date as an additional point of reference.

DAMAGED GOODS

If you receive a damaged gift, try to track down the retailer who sold the item. If this item didn't come from your registry, you'll need to let the gift giver know that the gift was delivered in a less-than-perfect condition. The gift giver might direct you to the store where the purchase was made or offer to exchange the gift for you. If she has the receipt, you'll be in a better position to confront the store in question.

If, on the other hand, you're forced to make an exchange without a receipt, be as firm as you can with the store's employees. You'll probably get only so far with them. They have no idea who you are, after all, and smaller stores often won't make returns or exchanges without a receipt.

THE PHANTOM GIFT

Occasionally a gift without a card—or *any* clue as to the identity of the giver—will arrive. That's when it's time to put your keen detective skills to work. If the gift arrived in the mail, check for the return address. No luck? Check to see whether the gift was purchased from the store where you're registered. If so, there might be a record of who bought it.

When it comes to gifts brought to the shower or reception, your job will be a little harder. Go through your guest list and try to figure things out by process of elimination. Whose gift is not accounted for? Worst-case scenario, if you hear (from your mother, most likely) that your Aunt Louise hasn't received a thank you note and you have absolutely no idea what she's given you, it's better to fudge a little on the thank you note than not to send one at all.

KEEPING UP WITH THANK YOU NOTES

With all of your wedding planning and other daily responsibilities to be done, it's going to be hard to keep up with thank you notes, especially if you're receiving loads and loads of gifts. Whenever possible, try to write the thank you note soon after you've receive a gift. It's better to do it in bits and pieces than to wait until it piles up all around you.

Try to be warm and personal in your thank you notes. Always mention the gift, and how you and your fiancé will be using it—this small touch will prevent people from feeling that you just sent them a form letter. (This, by the way, is completely unacceptable, no matter how busy you are!)

Keep in mind that writing a note for a cash gift is a little different than writing a note about a lamp. The specific monetary amount should not be mentioned in a thank you note; in the case of money, it's better to be vague and thank someone for their "very generous gift."

Registry and Gift-List Notes

Gifts for Your Wedding Party

. . . But enough about the gifts for you, already. While you're busy loving all of your new gifts, you've got some gift giving to do yourself. Giving your attendants gifts is the most popular way to say thank you for all the work, time, and money these kind souls put into your wedding. Have fun with it—this is your chance to play Santa to the people who matter most. After all, these people have been there for you through good times and bad. They've held your hand through every bad breakup, and held your hair back every time you got sick after stupidly drinking too much at a college party.

Now that you're getting married, your bridesmaids have probably searched high and low with you to find just the perfect dress—and tried to contain their laughter when looking at you in all of those not-so-perfect styles you tried along the way. And don't forget the groomsmen—if they talked your husband-to-be out of choosing a powder-blue ruffle tux that made him look like a refugee from a his high school prom, they're worth their weight in gold!

The care you take to choose a thoughtful gift means more than the money you spend. While some people choose to give their bridesmaids and groomsmen the same gift to avoid any resentment or hurt feelings, you can

Classic Concerns: Size Up Some Jewelry Options

Jewelry that matches your bridesmaids' dresses is always a great gift choice. If you want something really special, ask around or surf the Internet to find bead makers that create unique jewelry by hand. These options can be surprisingly affordable, and you'll be able to choose crystals or stones that match their gowns. Just be mindful that not everyone has pierced ears. Also, bracelets and necklaces can be tricky, because wrist and neck sizes vary. Take this into consideration when placing your order.

also individualize a little. Since these gifts are usually not given out until shortly before the wedding—often at the rehearsal dinner—you have time to shop around for just the right things. Set aside some time a month or two before the wedding to browse unusual gift stores or surf the Internet in search of just the right gifts. The time you take to add those personal touches will make the gifts all the more special.

You know your friends and family better than anyone else, so with a little thought you should be able to find something suitable for everyone. Don't forget the children in the wedding party (it's unlikely that a boy under fourteen would appreciate a shaving kit). When in doubt, most kids love gift certificates to their favorite toy store.

Don't Forget Your Parents!

In addition to gifts for their wedding party, some brides and grooms also give presents to their parents. If your parents were real troopers, standing beside you through every wedding-planning crisis that came along, whisking them off for a weekend away somewhere is a nice thought. Some rest and relaxation at a quaint bed-and-breakfast might be appropriate, or maybe an exciting trip to a nearby city is more their speed.

If you don't have enough money to send them away on a mini trip, there are plenty of other thoughtful things you can do. Consider tickets to a favorite concert or show, or perhaps dinner out at a great restaurant. Beautiful engraved frames or fancy photo albums are another good choice. You can either fill them ahead of time with special childhood photos, or save the space to hold wedding photos later on.

Even if your parents insist they don't need thanks because they love you and have been dreaming all their lives about your wedding day, thank them anyway. Everyone likes to feel appreciated.

Notes on the Attendants' Gifts

Celebrate with the Bridesmaids

An attendants' party gives you the chance to turn the tables—to honor the people who've been honoring (and assisting) *you*. It's a smart idea to have this party sometime during the week before the wedding, to give all the harried planners a chance to relax. And it gives you a chance to thank them for all that they have done for you during this busy time.

This may be the perfect time to give your attendants the gifts you've bought for them (if you want to wait till the rehearsal dinner, then that's fine, too). The guest list does not have to be limited to the attendants; family and close friends can be included also. To keep the atmosphere relaxed, consider having a brunch at home, a barbecue, a park picnic, lunch at a salon where you can all get your nails done, or a day at the beach. Make it a day (or night) to concentrate on what's up with your attendants' lives— you might have been missing out on some good stuff while you've been caught up in your own wedding whirlwind.

The Rehearsal

Who's going to plan it, who's going to pay for it, who's going to be invited? There are several details to consider for the rehearsal and its accompanying dinner. If you're expecting your wedding rehearsal to go something like the final dress rehearsal for a Broadway play, it probably won't. Chances are, you'll be excited but a little jittery. Don't worry about having a panic attack—your rehearsal won't be as nerve-wracking as you might think. The rehearsal is mainly a chance for your officiant to meet your wedding party and to acquaint everyone with the basics of the ceremony. This is your test run, so do it right!

Rehearsal Basics

The rehearsal is usually held the night before the wedding at the ceremony site itself. If that time is inconvenient for any of your key players, reschedule for some other point during the week before the wedding. (Just don't plan it too far in advance of the wedding—people might forget what they've learned.) Some couples also request rehearsal dates several nights before the wedding for logistical reasons. If you think you and your groom will be on edge or incredibly busy on the eve of the wedding itself, this might be the option for you.

THE SETTING

This section presents the rehearsal as it occurs when getting married in a church. Of course, you might be holding your ceremony in a gazebo in the park or on a rocky cliff. No matter—the procedure will be basically the same—you can easily adapt your rehearsal routine to fit your particular location and situation.

The most important thing is getting everyone comfortable with the setting and preparing them for the real thing. The location is secondary. In fact, you don't even have to practice at your actual ceremony location if that's not possible. Say you're getting married in a country club that's booked solid with parties the entire week before your wedding; you might not be able to have a rehearsal at the site. That's fine; simply gather everyone together and have a rehearsal anywhere space permits. All that really matters is that your participants have some idea of what the actual ceremony will be like, to ward off ceremony stage fright.

Classic Concerns: **Review Your Readings**

If you're a really on-the-ball bride, you're probably going to give your Scripture readers copies of their readings to practice ahead of time. Before you do, check with your officiant to make sure the version of Scripture you give them is, in fact, the one being used in the ceremony. Wording sometimes differs from Bible to Bible. Also verify that the Scripture selections you've made are definitely the ones that are ready for your ceremony—you don't want to be shocked as you stand at the altar listening to the wrong reading!

Bridesmaids' Luncheon Notes

THE PLAYERS

Who (besides you and your groom) should attend the rehearsal? That's easy: your officiant and basically anyone who's involved in your ceremony as more than just a guest. In addition to all of your bridesmaids and groomsmen, your parents and grandparents should be there to practice as part of the processional. Scripture readers, candle lighters, gift bearers, and any children taking part in the ceremony should all be included.

It's Show Time

The rehearsal is your chance to iron out last-minute details and resolve any remaining questions. Though it might not assuage your nerves completely, get everything straight at the rehearsal. Make sure everything is ready and that all of the participants know what's expected of them.

This is the time when your officiant makes sure everybody knows where to stand, what to do, and when to do it. After a brief overview of what's included in the ceremony, your officiant will talk everyone through a quick practice run, beginning with the processional, when your first bridesmaid takes her initial step down that long aisle.

MAIDS AND MEN IN A ROW

Your ceremony officiant will spend at least part of the rehearsal helping everyone to line up and then walk in and out of the ceremony properly.

Poised Under Pressure: You Can Take It with You

As you're getting yourself ready on the day of your wedding, you'll be too pre-occupied to remember certain things. Make sure you pack up a bag filled with all the stuff you need for your ceremony and bring it with you to rehearsal. Then, ask someone you trust to hand over the programs, unity candle, and anything else to your officiant for safekeeping and proper placement.

Classic Concerns: **Don't Agonize over Order**

How do you decide which best friend goes where, when they're all equally important to you? Don't give yourself an ulcer over this. Either pick names from a hat, or simply go back to sorting by height. There's nothing wrong with resorting to an arbitrary order.

Based on what you've already covered in the ceremony section, you have a pretty good idea of how this works. Except which bridesmaid leads the charge when you're ready to practice your entrance march? That's up to you. Some officiants might encourage you to line your maids up according to height; many brides like to keep their closest friends and family attendants near to them on the altar. For large weddings with many bridesmaids, send them down the aisle in pairs. The honor attendant is the last maid to walk down the aisle, followed by the ringbearer and flower girl. If your church has two side aisles instead of a single center aisle, your officiant will most likely advise you to use the left aisle for the processional and the right aisle for the recessional.

PLACES, PLEASE!

When you run through the ceremony, your musicians will most likely get off the hook (unless you arrange otherwise). Your readers and gift bearers are a different story, though. They should be ready to hit their marks. You and your groom will stand in your proper places as your officiant goes over the nuptials with you. He or she will remind you of the appropriate responses, and if you're going to be reciting your own vows, your officiant will let you know *when* you should speak.

Your officiant's directions might seem nit-picky at points (like when he tells you that you should be facing your groom more, or that you need to enunciate more clearly). Remember, he's in the know—after all, he has performed countless ceremonies. You might not know about the acoustical quirks in the place, but your officiant will know instantly whether the people in the third row will be able to hear you take your vows.

Your honor attendants will also be instructed on any special duties during the ceremony. (Your maid of honor will take your flowers at a certain point; your best man will present the rings.)

Once you're done running through the ceremony, you and your almost-husband will walk out arm in arm, just like on your wedding day, followed by your child attendants, your maid of honor and best man next, then pairs of your bridesmaids and groomsmen. And that's that. Now it's dinner time!

The Rehearsal Dinner: Your Last (Single) Supper

The rehearsal warms everyone up for the more enjoyable event of the evening: The rehearsal dinner and ensuing party. Hopefully, the rehearsal dinner gives everyone involved in the wedding a chance to start festivities off right and relax a bit before the big day. Once you leave the rehearsal site, forget about all your stress and quit giving your bridesmaids orders about the upcoming ceremony.

If after paying for your actual wedding you're concerned that there's not much money left over for rehearsal dinner, never fear. It doesn't have to be fancy. You can even extend rehearsal dinner invitations by phone to save yourself time and expense. Many of your guests will welcome a more casual event. Whether you have a catered or restaurant event, or host a backyard barbecue, pizza party, or potluck dinner, the important thing is that everyone gets to spend extra time together.

The Hosts and the Guests

Traditionally, the expense of the rehearsal party is borne by the groom's parents, but these days anyone who is up to the task can host the party. If you and your groom feel uncomfortable asking either set of parents to host this affair, or you want to plan it in conjunction with either or both sets of parents, go right ahead. Although you don't have to spend a lot, remember that this smaller gathering of guests includes those people who are closest to you—these guests shouldn't be expected to pay for anything.

Who should be invited? The absolute, bare minimum guest list should include:

- All members of the wedding party, along with their spouses or significant others. (This includes readers, gift bearers, and so on.)
- The parents and siblings of the bride and groom.
- The ceremony officiant, along with his or her spouse.
- Grandparents and godparents of the bride and groom.
- The parents of any child attendants.

Of course, you can invite anyone else you want (with your hosts' okay). If, for example, you're really close with your aunts and uncles, or you have good friends you couldn't manage to fit into the wedding party, invite them, too.

Classic Concerns: Remember the Out-of-Towners

Inviting your out-of-town guests to the rehearsal dinner is a great way to make them feel welcome. They'll feel like the trip was well worth it, and it shows them that you're really glad they could make it. The rehearsal dinner is actually the perfect time to touch base with out-of-town guests. You won't be as busy as you will be at the wedding so you'll actually have time for some complete conversations with your guests.

It's Better to Give . . .

Throughout your engagement, just about everyone who knows and loves you will be showering you with gifts and attention. The rehearsal is your chance to turn the tables. At the rehearsal dinner, brides and grooms usually hand out their gifts to the attendants, parents, and anyone else participating in the wedding. One suggestion here: Although you and your groom might also have wedding gifts for each other, it's a wise idea to wait on exchanging those until your wedding night or the honeymoon. Since you've both probably put a lot of thought into the gifts you've chosen, you want to take the time to enjoy their significance as well as read any special notes you've written each other.

Pour Your Heart Out

Even though plenty of speeches will probably be given at your actual wedding, there's a chance that some people might want to say a few words at the rehearsal dinner as well. Each set of parents might chime in, the groom might toast the bride and her family, the bride might respond with a toast to her groom and his family . . . . Of course, you're not being watched by the Etiquette Police here, so you're not bound to follow any sort of traditional order. If you prefer to skip the toasts altogether, that's fine, too. The important thing is that the sentiments expressed are spontaneous and heartfelt.

GETTING TO KNOW YOU

Weddings join not only two individuals, but two families and two circles of friends. Your rehearsal dinner is a perfect time for both sides to get acquainted. While everyone is mixing and mingling, set aside some time for guests to come forward and share a favorite story about the bride or groom. More than likely, the stories will keep your guests in stitches. You and your groom will also be touched as you hear about all the special things people in your life love about you. If you're not into the idea of formal toasts at your rehearsal dinner but you've got lots of eager guests just waiting to chime in about you, this works well.

Classic Rewind

Your rehearsal isn't just a time for everyone to learn the ins and outs of the ceremony; it's also your cue to let go. By the time you get to the rehearsal dinner, if you've done your job well, everything should be properly in place. Realize that there's only so much you can do to ensure that your wedding will run smoothly, and you've probably already done it. This is when you turn the specifics of your wedding day over to your ceremony officiant, reception coordinator, and vendors. Everyone needs to let loose a little right before the wedding. Don't be a Bossy Bride and begrudge your groom, your guests—or yourself—a good time.

Wrap-Up: Last-Minute Details in the Eleventh Hour

You're coming into the home stretch. Stay cool and keep it together—your wedding day is coming up on the horizon. Grab hold of some practical tips for organizing all of the last-minute details ahead of time so that you can breathe easy when your day finally arrives. The week before your wedding, you'll be the busiest you've ever been confirming details with vendors, setting aside the cash for all the wedding-day tips and fees; verifying the list of people you definitely want in photos, and so on. Above all else, *do not* continue to run around like a chicken with your head cut off right up until the moment the organist strikes up your bridal march. (Remember, you're shooting for grace and poise here.)

If you're insanely wound up just before your wedding, it will fly by even faster than you imagine. Pull all-nighters for a week straight if you have to as you finalize your seating chart and put the final touches on wedding favors, but make sure *everything* is organized and ready at least two or three days before the wedding. Then try as hard as you can to slow yourself down. In the days right before your wedding, spend as much time as you can decompressing and relaxing with your loved ones—it will help you to enjoy the entire experience to the fullest.

Rehearsal and Rehearsal Dinner Notes

Last-Minute Details

By this late date, no doubt, you've ironed out all of the logistical details for the big day. Still, there's something to be said for the kind of peace of mind that only comes with double (and even triple) checking. Following is a list of the things you'll need to attend to in the days just before your wedding.

◆ Reconfirm plans with your officiant, ceremony musicians, reception site coordinator, photographer, videographer, band or DJ, florist, baker, limousine company, and hair stylist. Make sure they know the correct locations and times.

◆ Reconfirm your honeymoon travel arrangements and hotel reservations; make sure all of the necessary documents and tickets are in order.

◆ Reconfirm your hotel reservation for your wedding night.

◆ Make sure your wedding attendants know where they need to be and when, and remind them of any special tasks they need to perform.

◆ Finish any last-minute packing.

◆ Pack a small wedding-night bag with a change of clothes, and any accessories and toiletries you'll need. If you'll be changing at your reception or hotel, put a friend in charge of making sure your stuff arrives there safely.

◆ Give your wedding rings and marriage license to your honor attendants to hold until the ceremony.

◆ Make sure your groom and best man have enough cash for tipping.

◆ Get your "emergency repair kit" ready and give it to a trusted attendant, so you'll be prepared to deal with the unexpected.

◆ Make sure your honeymoon luggage is ready to go and arrange to transport it ahead of time if it needs to get to the hotel where you're spending your wedding night.

◆ Arrange for a friend to drive your car to the reception site if you intend to drive yourselves to the hotel or inn where you'll be staying.

Poised Under Pressure: **Write a Cheat Sheet**

You probably don't want to think about this, but just what if your limo driver is late, or your photographer gets lost on the way to the reception? Rather than risk hysterics, write yourself a cheat sheet with important vendor telephone numbers, and carry it with you on the day of the wedding—this way, you'll have everything covered, just in case!

Your Happy Ending: The Wedding Day in Detail

With any luck, by the time the morning of your big day finally rolls around, you've spent some good quality bonding time with the girls at your bridesmaids' luncheon and you've had some extra time to mix and mingle with everyone at the rehearsal dinner. You should be full of excitement and ready to relish those final hours before you glide down the aisle. Here's how your day will go.

Up and at 'Em

Despite the fact that you checked your alarm clock ten times before you went to sleep, you're eyes probably popped open at the crack of dawn. (Presuming you actually did fall asleep the night before, rather than worry yourself straight out of dreamland.) All you need is a quick shower because there's probably no need to wash your hair before you get it done (day-old hair works better for fancy dos). The other good news is you don't have to fuss with your makeup because you've got your appointment with the cosmetologist later in the morning.

Jump into some jeans and don't forget to wear a button-down shirt so you won't wreck your hair once your veil is in place. No matter how jittery you're feeling, don't start the day's festivities without eating something first. You

Your Emergency Survival Bridal Box

Before *the big day rolls around, make up a box of items that you might need in an emergency. The essentials include:*

◆ *White tailor's chalk in case your gown gets dirty*

◆ *Safety pins in case the buttons come off the bustle*

◆ *Deodorant and baby powder*

◆ *Extra lipstick and any other makeup you'll need*

◆ *Gum and mints*

◆ *Extra perfume*

◆ *A spare pair of stockings*

◆ *More hairpins in case your veil gets loose or your hair starts to fall out (as if enough hairpins won't be stuck into your head already . . .)*

◆ *Tissues, for those moments when you can't stop the waterworks*

◆ *Clear Band-Aids (you do not want blood on the gown!)*

◆ *Wet wipes or moist towels, so if the day is hot and sticky, you can quickly freshen up in the ladies room*

need fuel to keep you from fainting as you walk down the aisle. Give yourself plenty of time to make any pit stops to pick up maids on the way to the hairdresser, and then prepare to have those tresses teased. Yes, you'll feel funny riding around afterward in your jeans and a veil, but just go with it.

Dress Up Time!

Proceeding according to schedule, you and the bridesmaids should arrive home with plenty of time to have your makeup done and get into your dresses. In an effort to keep your blood-sugar level in tip-top shape, your bridesmaids gently feed you snacks (so they don't ruin your makeup) as they fluff your veil and admire your dress. At some point during all of this preparation, your florist arrives with your bouquet and the bridesmaids' flowers. Some slight chaos ensues as the bridesmaids play musical rooms, vying for mirrors, bathroom space, and a place to put on their stellar sheaths. Meanwhile, your mother is trying to be patient as your father complains about how he can't get those darn cufflinks through the buttonholes even as she tries to make her way over to you to help you put on your gown.

Two hours before the ceremony, you start getting dressed. Brush on some baby powder first, so you'll stay fresh as you sweat under the spotlight later. (Keep that powder handy at all times; you'll need it.) Once you slip into your special undergarments, you call for help getting into your gown. Everyone else, including your mother, should be almost ready by now, so you have plenty of hands to fasten any tricky buttons or zippers. Once you're outfitted, you double-check that you have your "something old, something new, something borrowed, and something blue."

The photographer arrives at your house about an hour before the wedding to take shots of you alone, you with your family, and you with your attendants. The videographer might catch some of this fun, too, or she might already be busy at the ceremony taping guests as they enter. Across town, your groom is stepping out of the shower and into his tux. He takes a moment to call you before he heads out to the church, just to say hi. (With any luck, he conveniently leaves out the less-than-ideal details about that emergency tuxedo repair job at the formalwear shop and how he didn't sleep a wink the night before because the best man got sick from drinking too much.)

Poised Under Pressure: **Don't Be a Caffeine Spaz**

Avoid ingesting an overabundance of caffeine on your wedding day; you'll already be nervous enough, and coffee or soda might just push you over the edge into bridal insanity. It won't be a pretty sight . . .

Before you know it, the limo pulls up, your father helps you climb in, and you're whisked away to your ceremony site.

Give yourself more than enough time to accomplish everything you need to while getting ready the morning of your wedding. You don't want to be in such a hurry that you can't pause for a moment to enjoy as your bridesmaids snap photos of you getting your hair done or your mother laces up your gown. You'll hold those small instances in your memory every bit as much as you will the major events.

One final hint: Before you step into that limo and take off for your ceremony, pause for a second to be sure you have absolutely *everything* you need. You don't want to be without your lipstick—or worse, the rings—and then have to turn around and go back to get what you've missed.

Final Destination: The Honeymoon

You might not see it while you're embroiled in the chaos of wedding planning, but there is a light at the end of the tunnel, and it's called the honeymoon. This is what you have to look forward to after your big day. When all is said and done, you'll need more than just an ordinary vacation to recuperate from the anxiety, emotion, and excitement of your wedding. Your honeymoon is the perfect time to plan the vacation of your dreams.

There's more to plan for than just airfare and hotel accommodations. You'll need to arrange for passports and possibly vaccinations if you're traveling to a different country. Also be sure to sort other specifics. Are food and drinks included in your package, or do you have to budget in extra cash for those things? What about car rentals, train passes, taxi and parking fees? Don't forget spending money for things like souvenirs and entertainment. Plan well, plan in advance, and guess what? Once you arrive at your honeymoon destination, your poor planned-out body and mind won't have to plan another thing. You'll be done with everything, so just enjoy yourself. By then, you'll have earned it!

Your Grand Entrance

After fidgeting in the limo all by yourself for what seems like an eternity (but in reality probably only amounts to about ten minutes), everyone has been seated and you're ready to knock 'em dead. You gather in the vestibule and your bridesmaids line up, prepared to launch themselves down the aisle as the processional begins. You watch as one by one they start walking, as ordered, *very slowly*. Your father—and maybe your mother, too—takes your arm, and a bittersweet pang of emotion melts over you as you see the first tears slip down their cheeks.

You're elated as your parents give their blessing and your groom steps up to meet you at the altar. Then the ceremony begins, and it goes off without a glitch: officiant's greetings, reading, exchanging of rings, and kissing . . .

Classic Rewind

. . . And just like that, before you know it, you're married! *As you and your groom bounce down the aisle together and then make your way to the reception, you really will feel like you're living in a perfect dream. That's when you'll realize that all the crazy planning truly was worth it. Enjoy the day, but more importantly, enjoy your life together!*

Honeymoon Notes

Extra Notes

Extra Notes

Extra Notes

Extra Notes

Extra Notes

Extra Notes

Extra Notes